JOURNEY TO JESUS

Journey to Jesus

The Worship, Evangelism, and
Nurture Mission of the Church

Robert E. Webber

Abingdon Press
Nashville

JOURNEY TO JESUS
THE WORSHIP, EVANGELISM, AND NURTURE MISSION OF THE CHURCH

Copyright © 2001 by Abingdon Press

This book is printed on acid-free, recycled, elemental-chlorine–free paper.

Library of Congress Cataloging-in-Publication Data

Webber, Robert.
    Journey to Jesus: the worship, evangelism, and nurture mission of the church / Robert E. Webber.
        p. cm.
    Includes bibliographical references and index.
    ISBN 0-687-06840-1 (alk. paper)
    1. Public worship.   2. Evangelicalism.   3. Spiritual formation.   I. Title.

BV15 .W384 2001
266—dc21   2001053527

. 04 05 06 07 08 09 10—10 9 8 7 6 5 4 3 .

MANUFACTURED IN THE UNITED STATES OF AMERICA

Contents

IV. Equipping the Kneeler:
Mentoring the Maturing Believer

V. Incorporating the Faithful: Receiving
the New Member

Acknowledgments

No book is written apart from the input of many unknown as well as known sources. I owe a debt of gratitude to many people who have gone before. There are the church fathers who developed the early form of Worship, Evangelism, and Nurture from apostolic times. Then there are the numerous commentators on the Fathers whom I have cited in my notes and bibliography. I am fully aware of the rich treasury of tradition these primary and secondary writers represent. Without them this publication would not exist. I have written nothing creative nor innovative. I have simply adapted their work to our times.

There are also the known people without whom this book would not have been written. I thank the Abingdon staff in particular for visionary leadership, analytical skills, and attention to details. And then, there are my special friends and associates who have helped to birth this book. Sydney Westrate and Ashley Olsen helped enormously with the details of notes and bibliography, and Carmen Martinez has cheerfully typed and retyped draft after draft.

Last but not least is the support of my wife, Joanne, who is always willing to give me the time needed to write. Thanks to all!

Introduction

The model of evangelism proposed in this book is a resurrection of the seeker model of evangelism that originated in the third century (yes—the word "seeker" was used in the third century). I have translated and adapted this ancient approach to evangelism for today's church. It speaks particularly to the current search for an effective style of evangelism in a world dominated by postmodern thought, a church living in a post-Constantinian society, and the challenge to overcome the resurgence of pagan values.

I explained this model to my friend John, who is on the pastoral staff of a church in Minnesota. I asked: "How does this model strike you?" John thought for a moment and said, "It resonates with me. . . . The talk among my friends in ministry goes like this: 'We like the seeker concern, but we want to know, *is there a way to reach the seeker without the radical changes required by the seeker service model?*' The process you've described sounds like it could fill that need."

John summed up my pastoral intent. I want to restore the type of evangelism that resulted in the rapid spread of Christianity in the first three centuries, and I want to adapt this form of evangelism for use by any church committed to reaching seekers in the present post-Christian society (a world that bears striking similarity to the Roman Empire in its final centuries of decay and dissolution).

This approach to evangelism and nurture has the potential to answer current issues. Church leaders from every denomination and fellowship want to know how to take the widespread expressive individualism of the current turn toward spirituality and transform it into a constructive direction. How can we take the longing that so many people have for spiritual fulfillment and connect it with the Christian tradition of faith and spirituality? How do we form Christians? How do we generate Christian commitment? How do we communicate a sense of belonging to the community that is spread around the world today? This model of evangelism is designed to answer these questions.

What Does This Model of Evangelism Look Like?

- First, the *content* is grounded in the biblical and historical message of salvation through the person and work of Jesus Christ.
- Second, the *style* has the flexibility to be integrated into any type of setting.
- Third, the *structure* is characterized by *four stages of development and three passage rites* which mark the seeker's journey from conversion to a period of discipleship to a time for equipping the believer for spiritual warfare, finally, to incorporation into active church membership.

Churches that adopt this model can adapt it to work within their current worship services, calendar structures, and methods of assimilating new members. Many churches will find that my translation of the model will easily fit into their situation, but congregations are free to further customize this style in a way that works best for them.

1. Evangelism Old and New

In this chapter, I will

(1) describe the third-century form of evangelism.

(2) address the question of how this approach may be translated into our twenty-first-century situation.

(3) conclude with definitions of crucial terms that will be used throughout the book.

The Third-century Model of Evangelism

A chief source for our knowledge of evangelism in the early church is *The Apostolic Tradition*,[1] written around A.D. 215 by Hippolytus, a bishop in Rome. The ancient method of evangelism in the local church was a process, not a one-time decision made without a support community. This process brought a person to Christ and into full communion with the Christian community through periods of development and growth culminating in baptism. For example, the following phases of conversion are set forth in *The Apostolic Tradition:* (1) a time for Christian inquiry, known as the *seeker* period; (2) a time of instruction, when the converting person was known as a *hearer;* (3) an intense spiritual preparation for baptism, when the candidate was known as a *kneeler;* and (4) a time after baptism for incorporating the new Christian into the full life of the church, when the newly baptized person was known as *faithful.*

Each period of formation was set off by a passage rite that marked the transition to the next period of growth. These passage rites included (1) the rite of welcome into the church, (2) a rite of the enrollment of names, and (3) the rites that surround baptism. Consequently, early church evangelism consisted of four periods of growth framed by three passage rites. Here is a summary:

Phase I	Evangelism of the *seeker*
Passage Rite I	Welcome
Phase II	Discipleship of the *hearer*
Passage Rite II	Enrollment of Names
Phase III	Spiritual formation of the *kneeler*
Passage Rite III	Baptism
Phase IV	Nurturing of the *faithful* into full membership

This process was the primary form of evangelism on the eve of the conversion of the Roman Empire. After the conversion of Constantine, and the establishment of Christianity as the state religion by Emperor Theodosius in A.D. 380, the church lost its missional posture and was gradually accommodated to society. This change resulted in the demise of ancient evangelism.[2] Today, the death of Christendom in the West and the emergence of post-Christian culture and values mandates the return of the church to its missional status and to a recovery of the ancient practice of evangelism.[3]

How Can We Translate the Third-century Model into the Twenty-first Century?

I have chosen to maintain the ancient names of the four stages: *Seeker, Hearer, Kneeler,* and *Faithful.* As you read the text, you may read with the more contemporary names for these stages in mind: *Unchurched, New Believer, Maturing Believer,* and *New Member.*

We dare not extract the ancient model of evangelism from its setting in the Roman Empire and transplant it without any modification. Although this book is based on the ancient model, it adapts its style, spirit, and essence for the twenty-first century. I have followed the principle of re-presentation suggested by postmodern philosopher Hans-George Gadamer.[4] His idea is that "we are able to re-present an original presentation in a different paradigm in such a way that the re-presented content remains faithful to the spirit of the original, even though the cultural setting and the language forms of the new paradigm are somewhat different."[5] This is called the fusion of horizons.

This book "fuses" the ancient process of worship, evangelism, and nurture into the twenty-first-century culture. This is possible because our culture bears great similarity to the ancient pagan setting in which Christianity spread so rapidly and overcame paganism. This current translation takes into account the cultural situation of postmodern thought, post-Constantinian society and neo-pagan values. It draws on the current recovery of ancient theology, ecclesiology, missiology, spirituality, and symbology as well as premodern views of stages of growth and development. A brief overview of the contents of *Journey to Jesus* will help us see how this translation has been made between the two paradigms of history.

- In chapter 1, I introduce evangelism in the early church and show how it may be translated into the post-Christian world.
- In the first section, I deal with the crucial issue of a missional church in a pagan culture. Chapter 2 examines the cultural situation of the pre-Constantinian period. It then asks: how did the church do evangelism

in this situation? Chapter 3 compares our current culture to premodern culture and argues for a recovery of the ancient form of evangelism. Chapters 2 and 3 are foundational because they set forth the pagan culture old and new, and place the missional church in the context of a post-Christian culture.

- The remaining sections deal with the four phases of evangelism and nurture as they unfold from one phase to the next. In each of the phases the evangelism of the ancient church is presented. Then I deal with its current adaptation, and conclude by showing how the passage rite moves the converting person into the next phase of spiritual growth.
- In the first phase I deal with *evangelizing the seeker (unchurched)*. This section ends with the rite of conversion.
- In the second phase I discuss *how to disciple the hearer (new believer)*. The rite of covenant ends the section.
- In the third phase I look at *equipping the kneeler (maturing believer)* to deal with spiritual warfare. It ends with the rite of baptism.
- In the final phase I focus on the process of *incorporating the faithful (new member)* into the church. It ends with the rite of the Eucharist (Lord's Supper) as a continual rite of spiritual nourishment.
- The final chapter presents several models of application for use in the post-Christian world.

I refer to the four phases of this process of the converting person as *Journey to Jesus*. This name captures the current interest in spirituality and speaks to the process of Christian growth and maturity. The chart below summarizes the four phases of spiritual development, showing the purpose of each one, the worship rite that serves as a transition into the new phase, and the resource booklet that may be used to evangelize, disciple, equip, and incorporate the new Christian into the church:

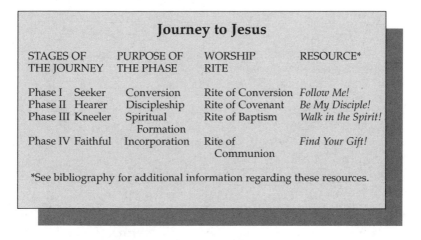

Journey to Jesus			
STAGES OF THE JOURNEY	PURPOSE OF THE PHASE	WORSHIP RITE	RESOURCE*
Phase I Seeker	Conversion	Rite of Conversion	*Follow Me!*
Phase II Hearer	Discipleship	Rite of Covenant	*Be My Disciple!*
Phase III Kneeler	Spiritual Formation	Rite of Baptism	*Walk in the Spirit!*
Phase IV Faithful	Incorporation	Rite of Communion	*Find Your Gift!*

*See bibliography for additional information regarding these resources.

Defining Crucial Terms

Throughout the book I assume the reader understands the concepts behind postmodern thought and post-Constantinian society, and I address neo-pagan values directly.[6] I also use two other terms: *the mission of God (Missio Dei)* and *the missional church*. Brief discussions of these concepts and terms are listed below.

Postmodern Thought

Today's world no longer sees the world in terms of modern categories. Therefore it is called postmodern. In the modern world, Christians interpreted Christianity using the dominant categories of science and reason. Science and reason, coupled with the empirical methodology of gathering facts, analyzing them, and systematizing them into propositions, led the church into a highly rationalistic Christianity.

This rational approach to Christianity produced an "apologetic" Christianity. Evangelists attempted to show that science and reason supported the faith. Books like *Evidence That Demands a Verdict,* by Josh McDowell, were very popular. Evangelism based on tracts like "Four Things God Wants You to Know" or "The Four Spiritual Laws" were used by many committed to evangelism, and were popular ways to present Christianity.

Because of the new revolutions in science and philosophy, there is wide skepticism about the modern rational approach to Christianity. At present, many theologians argue that we should never have been reliant on science and reason. Likewise, many Christian leaders argue that the church must return to classical Christianity. For example, John Milbank has created a worldwide theological stir with his argument that instead of interpreting Christianity through reason and science, we ought to turn the table and interpret science and reason through Christianity. He calls for a return to Scripture interpreted by the Fathers of the church and summarized in the great ecumenical creeds of the ancient church. Milbank writes: "Consider, for example, the doctrine of the incarnation. . . . all history before Christ can be narrated as 'anticipating' his story, and all history since as situated within it. . . . This, then, is to treat Christ as 'measuring' all reality, in the same way that God's generated wisdom, his word, is taken to do." [7]

I do not want to oversimplify Milbank and the complexity of his thought. I only hope to point out that postmodern Christianity is returning to the foundations of Christianity shaped by the early church. Here we have the truth about life handed down to us in the communal life of the church, especially in the church's worship where the story of faith is proclaimed and enacted. This new theological thrust takes us back to the common roots of our faith in the early church. It says, *You do not interpret Christianity through the world, but the world through Christianity.* This book is written from the perspective of a postmodern adaptation of classical Christianity and suggests that new Christians be formed by a Christian faith consistent with the biblical and historic tradition.

Post-Constantinian Society

A second significant change that occurred at the end of the twentieth century is the demise of Christendom. Christendom can be defined as the notion of a Christian society or, at the very least, a society dominated by Christian ideals. The idea of Christendom was birthed in the fourth century when Roman emperor Constantine was converted. The church set about to create the kingdom of God *on earth*. By A.D. 380, the emperor Theodosius proclaimed Christianity to be the only legitimate religion in the Roman Empire. His idea of a Christian society was a struggle to achieve, but was most closely accomplished in the thirteenth century, the golden era of Catholicism, when the church ruled society. The goal of a Christian society remained the ideal of the Reformers (minus the Anabaptists). It shaped the culture of modern Europe, it was a motivating factor for the Puritans, and it was the ideal of many who came to America to achieve the freedom of religion.

During modern Christendom, the American church has generally been seen as a servant of the political order. It played the role of "chaplain to society" and acted as "priest over national events," creating a "civil religion" that was sometimes a veneer of Christianity. Today a cacophony of voices are calling us to recognize that the church is not the servant of world politics. The church serves the political victory of God over the powers of evil through the life, death, and resurrection of Jesus Christ. For example, Stanley Hauerwas and William Willimon write: "A tired old world has ended, an exciting new one is awaiting recognition. This book is about a renewed sense of what it means to be Christian, more precisely, of what it means to be pastors who care for Christians, in a distinctly changed world."[8] Like these writers, I argue for evangelism that goes back to Scriptures and draws from the early church, a view of evangelism *before* the church became politicized. In a *post*-Constantinian world, we should recover *pre*-Constantinian evangelism rather than perpetuate Constantinian forms of evangelism that are not effective in a post-Christian world.

Neo-Pagan Values

Prior to the conversion of Constantine, the church functioned in a pagan culture. Christianity was one of numerous religions in a world that was highly religious but amoral. Pagans had little sense of right and wrong and placed very little value on life. (For example, the devaluation of humanity was expressed through the infanticide of female babies.)[9] Pagan culture was also a world of the occult, Satanism, magic arts, and astrology. We live, work, worship, and evangelize in a neo-pagan world, a world of "after virtue," as Alasdair MacIntyre has written.[10] In this world, pagan religion flourishes. Margot Adler writes:

> The thousands of people in the United States today who call themselves Pagans or Neo-Pagans use the word *pagan* in a very different way. These people . . . consider themselves part of a religious movement that antedates Christianity and monotheism. *By pagan* they usually mean the pre-Christian nature religions of the West, and their own attempts to revive them or to re-create them in new forms. The modern Pagan resurgence includes the new feminist goddess-worshipping groups, certain new religions based on the visions of science-fiction writers, attempts to revive ancient European religions—Norse, Greek, Roman—and the surviving tribal religions.[11]

Her book is the story of the *resurgence* of neo-paganism in today's world, a very real and troublesome presence.

The cultural situation of the current church is much like the culture in which Christianity emerged in the first three centuries—competing religions, a marginalized church, pagan values. So we ask, *What was the message of the early church in this setting? How did the early church evangelize in this culture? What can we learn from the message and method of the early Christians?*

The Message: Missio Dei

Throughout this book I will refer to the *mission of God*— God's work to rescue the world from the powers of evil through the work of Jesus Christ (John 3:16).[12] This was the vision of the early church, a vision, I argue, that needs to be recovered in our post-Christian society.

In sum, this vision teaches that God created a good world, and created men and women for fellowship and to express the glory of God in their work of caring for the world (Gen. 2:15). Conflict between good and evil entered the world through the fallen powers of evil (Gen. 3:1-24). Because of the Fall, Adam and Eve lost their relationship with God and ceased to do their work under God. Their fallen condition became reflected in their culture making. Society eventually became full of violence, hate, greed, war, and the like (Genesis 4–11). God determined to rescue the world (Gen. 12:1-3). In order to accomplish God's purposes, God became involved in human history. In God's involvement with Israel, we see types and shadows of what is to come. In the incarnation of God in Jesus Christ and by his life, death, and resurrection, God rescues the world from the powers of evil (see the Christ hymns John 1:1-14, Phil. 2:6-11, Col. 1:13-22). Jesus is the second Adam who reverses what resulted from the first Adam's rebellion against God—sin and death. Jesus, through his life, sacrificial death (Hebrews 7–9), and resurrection (1 Corinthians 15), won a victory over the powers of evil (Col. 2:13-15). At the end of history, the powers will be destroyed and Jesus Christ will reign forever in the new heavens and the new earth (Rom. 8:18-25; Revelation 20–21). God has won the war over evil, so that "at the name of Jesus every knee should bend, in heaven and on earth and under the earth, and every tongue should confess that Jesus Christ is Lord, to the glory of God the Father" (Phil. 2:10-11). Relationship with God is reestablished. In light of this truth, we ask the second question: What is the work of the church?

The Missional Church

The purpose of the church in God's world is to embody the Christian message, to proclaim it, to enact it, and to anticipate God's eschatological rule when all will be under the reign of Christ. In brief, the church is a "witness" to God's mission.[13] This "work of the church" is

- to embody in *community* what a redeemed people can look like (Acts 2:42-47).
- to witness to the world that the powers of evil have been defeated (Eph. 3:10).
- to call the world to live under the reign of Jesus Christ who is Lord of creation (Gal. 1:15–2:10).
- to go and tell the world the good news (Acts 1:8).
- to call the world to repent, be baptized, receive the Holy Spirit (Acts 2:38).
- to invite all to live in the fellowship of God's new community (Eph. 2:19-22).
- to enlist the world in expectation of Christ's coming to set up his kingdom and rule forever (2 Pet. 3:10-18).
- to model living exemplary lives (2 Pet. 3:14).

To summarize, the church is seen as a *historical* people connected to the past and having a memory of God's work in history. The church is also as an *eschatological* people who know the future and are called to live now under the reign of Jesus Christ. The work of the church in the *present* is to be a community of memory and hope. In this way the church tells and shows the world the truth about itself. The world only knows the truth about its origins, its meaning, and its end from the church. Therefore the church does not want to rule the world, or be the chaplain of the world, or try to accomplish its purposes in the world by aligning itself with a particular political party. Rather, the church is simply about the politics of Jesus—joyfully proclaiming to the whole world the good news that the powers have been defeated and that Jesus is Lord. "Come," says the church, "follow Jesus: be discipled by God's earthly community, be equipped to do warfare with the powers of evil, and experience a spiritual life in God's expectant community here on earth." This is the message the church celebrates in its worship, proclaims in its evangelism, and nurtures in its pastoral care. I call it the "worship, evangelism, and nurture mission" of the church. This book calls for a recovery of that message as the mission of the church for the present and future.[14]

How to Use and Read This Book

Journey to Jesus can be used in two ways. First, this process is primarily to *evangelize the seeker* and oversee his or her maturing relationship with Jesus Christ in the church through discipleship, spiritual formation, and incorporation into the church as a new member. These phases, with the transitional rites of conversion, covenant, and baptism, represent a journey of faith that "starts" the new Christian on a lifelong journey to Jesus. (This process can also be used as a journey for children of believers who are preparing for baptism, or for confirmation in churches that practice infant baptism).

The second way this process can be used in the local church is as a ministry tool to *revitalize the congregation.* Some congregations are not ready to do outreach. One way to prepare a congregation to become an evangelizing community is to walk through the entire *Journey to Jesus* process with a core group of people. This group will "gain a sense" of the process and then become the primary evangelists as the church promotes the *Journey to Jesus* for all members. The process can also be used by lapsed Christians who wish to revitalize their own faith and return to the full life of the church.

Finally, a word needs to be said about how to read this book. Some will want to read it out of historical curiosity. How the early church evangelized is a matter of great interest. The notes and bibliography will lead the reader to many helpful studies in the field of history, theology, education, spirituality, and evangelism. However, my intention in writing this book is pastoral. I believe in the model and think it is theologically sound, historically tested, and highly relevant to our post-Christian setting. Therefore my hope is that you will read with an eye toward implementing this form of evangelism in your church. As you read continually ask: *What will it take for my congregation to do this kind of evangelism?*

The *Worship, Evangelism, and Nurture Mission* is pertinent to our culture—the longing for a credible spirituality, the desire for community, and the demand for authenticity. The process can be done with simplicity, grace, and power. This is not a program or technique, but an unfolding process that works naturally to order and organize the experience of conversion, entrance into the church, and spiritual depth. The process has the potential to revive an entire congregation, since it draws people together by means of a common goal. Moreover, it energizes congregations that have become spiritually tired. It quickens faith, deepens spirituality, releases the gifts of all the people and grows the congregation numerically and in depth. My hope is that you will read the book to gain a new vision for the church in its inner life and in its outreach.

In order to help you implement the *Worship, Evangelism,*

and Nurture Mission, the end of each chapter contains a Leader's Guide that asks you to evaluate the present practices of your congregation and to think through a course of constructive action for the revitalization of the local church and for outreach. In addition, a suggested list of resources is provided for further reading and study.

Leader's Guide

A. EVALUATE
   1. How effective is your current approach to evangelism?
   2. How well do you understand the current climate of a post-Christian society?

B. PLANNING A COURSE OF ACTION
   TO REVITALIZE THE CONGREGATION
   Ask the following:
   • What is going on in our culture?
   • Is this church listening to our culture?
   • Are we being called by God to do the *Worship, Evangelism, and Nurture Mission?*
   • Should a group of our people travel the *Journey to Jesus* to revitalize our community, or are we ready to do the outreach dimension of the *Worship, Evangelism, and Nurture Mission?*

C. PLANNING A COURSE OF ACTION FOR
   OUTREACH
   Ask the following:
   • Who would we appoint to be the pastor of spiritual formation to provide leadership to our outreach?

- How would we present this process to the congregation?
- How will we identify the people willing to be involved?
- When should we start?
- Should we have a commissioning service for the volunteer evangelist?

Resources for Further Reading

For a helpful introduction to evangelism in the early church read Michel Dujarier, *The Rites of Christian Initiation* (New York: Sadlier, 1979). In order to understand the contemporary culture of postmodern thought, read Jean-Francois Lyotard, *The Postmodern Condition* (Minneapolis: University of Minnesota Press, 1997), and Margot Adler, *Drawing Down the Moon: Witches, Druids, Goddess-Worshippers, and Other Pagans in America Today* (New York: Penguin, 1997).

I
The Missional Church

JOURNEY TO JESUS

FAITHFUL

Spiritual Goal:
  Incorporation
Continuous Rite:
  Eucharist
Resource:
  Find Your Gift!

KNEELER

Spiritual Goal:
  Spiritual
  Formation
Passage Rite:
  Rite of Baptism
Resource:
  *Walk in the
  Spirit!*

HEARER

Spiritual Goal:
  Discipleship
Passage Rite:
  Rite of
  Covenant
Resource:
  Be My Disciple!

SEEKER

Spiritual Goal:
  Conversion
Passage Rite:
  Rite of
  Conversion
Resource:
  Follow Me!

INTRODUCTION

St. Mark's in downtown Philadelphia is an old stone church squeezed in among a row of refurbished colonial homes and shops. There I went on a mission that was destined to affect me more than it did the people of St. Mark's. My task during a Friday evening service was to speak on evangelism then conduct a workshop on the subject the following Saturday morning.

What the congregation expected or even wanted from me was not clear. I only knew this was a church interested in reaching its neighborhood with the gospel. In preparation for the workshop, I found myself returning to an idea born of a conversation with an evangelical leader, to whom I had given the Book of Common Prayer *as a gift. After reading it, he came to me and declared, "Why, there is more gospel in the* Book of Common Prayer *than you will find in a typical church in a month of Sundays."*

No one will dispute that the worship of the church, whether Catholic, Orthodox, Anglican, Lutheran, or other denomination, is filled with the gospel. The gospel is present in the prayers, Scripture readings, Apostles' Creed, kiss of peace, and supremely in the Eucharist. At the table of the Lord, the gospel is not only verbalized, but also dramatized in the physical symbols of bread and wine.

My theme, which was "The Gospel in Worship," developed this idea: "Here in your hands you hold the greatest gift for evangelism and renewal available to your church." I elaborated on this theme by showing how the weekly celebration of worship proclaims and reenacts the death and resurrection of Jesus Christ for the renewal of the world.

My experience at St. Mark's helped me understand why the

27

principles of ancient evangelism and nurture need to be adapted for use in today's postmodern world.

In this section I look first at the cultural situation of the ancient missional church and then show how the cultural situation of today's church is similar. The question we will ask is, What was the message of the church then and what should it be now?

2. The Missional Church in the Ancient World

To understand evangelism in the ancient church we must

(1) examine the church's cultural situation in the Roman Empire;
(2) probe the church's self-understanding; and
(3) look at the church's missional theology of evangelism, as a way of illustrating how the message and method of evangelism was effective in a pagan world.

The Cultural Situation of the Ancient Church

During its first three centuries, the church existed in the Roman Empire. From the beginning, the Roman government was hostile toward the church because the church proclaimed Christ as Lord and refused to bow to the emperor as lord.[1] During this time of extreme conflict between Christ and culture, the church originated and grew.

In Rome, religion existed to serve the state. The Romans believed that as long as the gods were pleased with the worship of the people, they would bless the empire. Consequently, the Romans attributed the peace and prosperity of their empire to the gods and encouraged their people to be religious.

But religion was in the hands of the Roman senate, and only those gods that had been approved by the senate could be worshiped. As the empire expanded and people from all over the Mediterranean moved to Rome, the diversity of religions increased greatly. In order to establish some kind of unity between these religions, the Romans instituted a new cult centered in the person of the emperor. Everyone was required to recognize the emperor as deity. This term *deity* meant that the Roman emperor was to be worshiped as "the giver of good things." The Romans were to give honor and praise to the emperor as the *symbol* of the gods who gave prosperity to Rome and made it great. Consequently, the names of most of the traditional gods of Rome were attached to the emperor cult.

The circumstances in which Christianity was born and grew, then, were rather difficult. The state was in itself a religion; and in order to participate in the state, one needed to recognize its religious character, especially as symbolized in the emperor. This the Christian could not do. The natural result was an increasing tension between the church and Rome.[2]

Several factors heightened the tension between church and state. Because Christianity began as a Jewish movement, and since the Jews were already out of favor with the Romans, it was natural for the Romans to transfer hatred from the Jews to Jewish Christians. Like the Jews, Christians could not produce an image of their God; and, like the Jews, they denied the existence of all gods except their own. The Romans concluded from this that Christians were "atheists." It was also rumored that Christian worship consisted of some form of cannibalism. They ate the "body" and the "blood" of the "Son." The gossip of Rome was that Christians met in secret, butchered babies, ate their flesh, drank their blood, and ended their meeting with orgies. Given these misconceptions, Romans believed that Christians were immoral.

The Christians' anticipation of the coming kingdom of Christ and his rule over the world added to their notoriety in the Roman Empire. Christian apocalyptic hopes anticipated the destruction of all empires, the downfall of Rome, and the setting up of Christ's kingdom. News of this sort struck fear into the hearts of the Roman rulers and caused the Romans to look on Christians as political anarchists. Because of these misgivings about Christianity, the church could not be in favor with the Roman government.

Persecution against the Christians began in the first century under Nero, and by the turn of the century had spread to other parts of the Roman Empire. But the persecutions were sporadic and local until the third century. At that point, several factors prompted a more systematic attempt to rid the empire of the Christians. For one thing, the fortunes of the empire had decreased, and since the worship of the gods was regarded as integral to the continued prosperity of the state, it was thought that the gods were displeased and that they expressed their displeasure in the declining prosperity and stability of the Roman Empire. The widespread popularity of Christianity among the people made it suspect. Perhaps the gods were unhappy with the negative influence of these atheistic, immoral, revolutionary people. Given these conditions and the fact that Christians supported the coming kingdom of Christ, an intensified persecution against them was undertaken by Decius in the middle of the third century.

A group known as the Apologists defended Christianity against the charges brought against it. Against the accusation of immorality, the apologists asserted that the morality of Christians strengthened the fabric of Roman society. Theophilus, in his letter to Autolycus, reminded Autolycus that with Christians "temperance dwells, self-restraint is practiced, monogamy is observed, chastity is guarded, iniquity exterminated, sin extirpated, righteousness exercised, law administered, worship performed, God acknowledged."[3] The philosopher Aristides wrote: "They do not commit adultery nor fornication, nor bear false witness, nor covet the things of others. . . . They are eager to do good to their enemies; they are gentle and easy to be entreated. . . . [They] live holy and just lives, as the Lord enjoined upon them."[4]

31

Apologists also refuted the charge that Christians were revolutionaries about to overthrow the Roman government. The apologists pointed out that Christians believed the government functioned by divine sanction. Christians stood in the tradition of Paul, who wrote that "everyone must submit himself to the governing authorities" (Rom. 13:1 NIV), and of Peter, who likewise insisted that Christians "submit yourselves for the Lord's sake to every authority instituted among men: whether to the king, as the supreme authority, or to governors, who are sent by him to punish those who do wrong and to commend those who do right" (1 Pet. 2:13-14 NIV).

In his work *Against Heresies,* Irenaeus summed up the general attitude of Christians toward the Roman government. He wrote that it was God who has "appointed the kingdoms of this world" that "God imposed upon mankind the fear of man, as they did not acknowledge the fear of God, in order that, being subjected to the authority of men, and kept under restraint by their laws, they might attain to some degree of justice, and exercise mutual forbearance through dread of the sword."[5] Nevertheless, the early Christians looked on government as a "human institution" established as a result of the Fall. Consequently, government would not be needed in the new heavens and the new earth. And so far as government here on earth was concerned, it could not become Christian. For that reason early Christians, like their spiritual ancestors, were "looking forward to the city with foundations, whose architect and builder is God" (Heb. 11:10 NIV).

The Missional Church's Eschatological Understanding

Christians understood themselves as an eschatological people. They were informed by the vision of Peter, who said they should "look forward to the day of God and speed its coming. That day will bring about the destruction of the heavens by fire, and the elements will melt in the heat" (2 Pet. 3:12 NIV). Their eschatology was also informed by Paul's teaching, that "the creation itself will be liberated from its bondage to decay and brought into the glorious freedom of the children of God" (Rom. 8:21 NIV). The early church father Irenaeus taught that it was neither the substance nor the essence of creation that would pass away, but the *fashion* of the world:

> But when this [present] fashion [of things] passes away, and man has been renewed, and flourishes in an incorruptible state, so as to preclude the possibility of becoming old, [then] there shall be the new heaven and the new earth, in which the new man shall remain, always holding fresh converse with God.[6]

This eschatological vision established the Christians' vision of a perfect society in the future. The idea that the perfect kingdom of God could be realized on earth was quite foreign to the ancient Christian mind. We see this eschatological self-understanding reflected in their view of government and in their view of Christian involvement in a pagan society.

First, Christian loyalty to the vision of the future kingdom of God did not mean that Christians were anarchists or disloyal to the state. The Fathers made it very clear that Christians did not have the right to rebel against the government. Christians, according to Justin, were taught civil obedience by Christ and were therefore to be accounted among the best citizens: "And everywhere we, more readily than all men, endeavor to pay to those appointed by you the taxes both ordinary and extraordinary."[7] Therefore, Justin continued, "to God alone we render worship, but in other things we gladly serve you, acknowledging you as kings and rulers of men, and praying that with your kingly power you be found to possess also sound judgment."[8]

Second, because of their eschatological vision Christians

recognized they were to live lives that were different. The *Didache*, the earliest Christian manual of behavior, begins by saying, "They are two ways, one of life and one of death; and between the two ways there is a great difference."[9] There follows a detailed description of how the Christian is to live, what he is to do and what he is to refrain from doing. This document is only one of many that give us insight into what it means to live out of an eschatological vision. For example, Christians generally refused to be involved in vocations that demanded an allegiance to Caesar. Government officials and workers in the New Testament period became Christians and apparently stayed in these positions.[10] But by the end of the second century, involvement in the military and civil service was avoided. Hippolytus indicates that a person who is in military service and becomes a Christian may remain, but "if a cate-chumen or a believer seeks to become a soldier, they must be rejected, for they have despised God."[11] A similar attitude was taken toward civil service. Hippolytus insists that a "civic magistrate that wears the purple must resign or be rejected [from the church]."[12] Magistrates who wore the purple were continually expected to pronounce and inflict capital punishment. They were also involved in the support of emperor-worship. Tertullian summarized the attitude of the early church by insisting that "there is no agreement between the divine and the human sacrament [oath], the standard of Christ and the standard of the devil, the camp of light and the camp of darkness. One soul cannot be true to two *masters*—God and Caesar."[13]

Because of their commitment to be an eschatological people, ancient Christians took a dim view of involvement in pagan society. For example, the early Christians expressed a negative view toward Roman entertainment because so much of it involved killing (for example, as seen in the movie *Gladiator*). Consequently, those who desired to become converts and full members of the church were instructed to have nothing to do with gladiatorial exhibitions. They were warned against the circus and other shows because of idolatry and the display of immorality. Tertullian insisted that "we lapse from God . . . by touching and tainting ourselves with the world's sins" by "going as a spectator to the circus and theatre," for "the polluted things pollute us."[14] Athenagoras warns against the shows because "to see a man put to death is much the same as killing him."[15]

But the eschatological witness of the early church was not entirely negative. Christians exerted a strong positive influence on society by their concern for upright living. Even pagan critic Lucian observed, "It is incredible to see the ardor with which the people of that religion help each other in their wants. They spare nothing. Their first legislator [Jesus] has put into their heads that they are all brethren."[16] The following examples illustrate the positive influence exerted by early Christians on society.

First, Christians were willing to share their wealth. Their attitude toward possessions evidenced itself in Jerusalem, where "no one claimed that any of his possessions was his own, but they shared everything they had. . . . There were no needy persons among them. For from time to time those who owned lands or houses sold them, brought the money from the sales and put it at the apostles' feet, and it was distributed to anyone as he had need" (Acts 4:32-35 NIV). This attitude continued in the early church. Justin Martyr wrote, "We who valued above all things the acquisition of wealth and possessions, now bring what we have into a common stock, and communicate to every one in need."[17] Each congregation had a common fund to which all contributed for the benefit of the needy.

Second, the Christian spirit of hospitality evidenced itself in the attitude taken toward the sick, the poor, and the homeless. The classical world had displayed very little concern for the needy. Plato, for example, thought that allowing the poor to die would shorten their misery. Ancient society even allowed orphans to be raised for prostitution. Christians, by contrast, were concerned about the poor, active in hospitality to the stranger, and cared for orphans and castaway children.

Third, Christians also took a more humane approach toward slavery. Most slaves were originally captured soldiers whose lives were in the hands of their owners. In the second century, a series of laws made conditions for slaves more tolerable. The slaves were able to accumulate enough wealth to buy their own freedom. Historical evidence shows that Christians also owned slaves but regarded them in a kindly way: Paul admonished Philemon to take Onesimus back not as a slave, but as a beloved brother (Philemon 16). Aristides informs us that "if one or another of them have bondmen and bondwomen or children, through love towards them they persuade them to become Christians, and when they have done so, they call them brethren without distinction."[18] The church encouraged the release of slaves and even had a liturgy for the occasion. It was also not uncommon for a slave owner to set a number of slaves free on the day of his baptism. Many Christian slaves were also active in the church. In A.D. 220, Collistus, who had been a Christian slave, became bishop of Rome.

Fourth, Christians also had a positive effect on society through their emphasis on sexual morality and stable marriages. At a time of heightened moral negligence and the demolition of family structure, Christians insisted on high moral standards. As the author of the Epistle to Diognetus said, "They marry, like everyone else. . . . They share their board with each other, but not their marriage bed."[19]

The pre-Constantinian church understood the church's mission through eschatology. For early Christians, mission formed a people who embodied God's future redemption. By its very existence the church witnessed to the overthrow of evil and to the coming kingdom of God. This witness to

God's victory over the powers of evil was reflected in their process of evangelism that flourished in the third and fourth centuries, prior to the conversion of Constantine and during the most intense time of persecution by the state. Their theology of evangelism was to first turn people away from their commitment to all that was sin and death and second to bring them into Christ and his church, the people who lived as a witness to the eschatological rule of Christ over all. We turn now to examine the theology of evangelism that emerged from their eschatological self-understanding.

The Theology of Evangelism in the Early Church

Four themes emerge as the most distinguished marks of the ancient church which engaged in worship, evangelism, and nurture. They are as follows:

(1) the warfare theme of *Christus Victor*
(2) the nurturing theme of the *church as mother*
(3) the understanding that conversion and entrance into the full life of the church is a *process*
(4) the importance of *performative symbol* as a visible expression of conversion into Christ and the church.

These themes all reflect the eschatological self-understanding of the church and express its approach to evangelism in a hostile and pluralistic society.

First, the ancient evangelism process is characterized by the theme of *Christus Victor*.[20] *Christus Victor* implies Christ as Lord of the universe as opposed to other worldly or spiritual powers. By proclaiming "Jesus is Lord," a person also announced that "Caesar is not Lord," hence placing his or her own life in jeopardy. This theme is captured in an early Easter sermon preached by Melito, the bishop of Sardis. He concludes with these words:

> I, he says, am the Christ.
> I am the one who destroyed death,
> and triumphed over the enemy,
> and trampled Hades under foot,
> and bound the strong one,
> and carried off man
> to the heights of heaven,
> I, he says, am the Christ.[21]

The theme of *Christus Victor* is also central in the liturgy of the Eucharist. The earliest known eucharistic prayer comes from Hippolytus in A.D. 215 According to Hippolytus, the general themes of the prayer go all the way back to his childhood. In this prayer we find these *Christus Victor* words: "When he was betrayed to voluntary suffering that he might destroy death, and break the bonds of the devil, and tread down hell."[22]

The entire process of salvation, as you will see in future chapters, is based on the conviction that by his sacrifice Christ has defeated the powers of evil. Conversion to Christ is a turning away from an allegiance to evil and choosing to be under the reign of Christ. This theme is reflected in baptism. As the converting person stands in the water he or she is asked to show a sign of the rejection of the devil. The convert turns to the west (the symbol of the domain of Satan) and spits as in the face of the devil. A powerful way to symbolize the end of a relationship! This practice is continued in the Orthodox church today. For example, one of my students was baptized into an evangelical church of the Antiochene Orthodox Mission. I attended the baptism and watched intently as the minister asked her, "Pachomius, do you reject the devil and all his works?" After she answered with a firm "yes," the minister said, "Show us a sign." Pachomius tuned abruptly toward the west, the symbolic domain of Satan, and proceeded to spit as in the face of the devil. This is a powerful performative symbol that should live in a Christian's memory and form her continual opposition to the powers of evil.

The second theological theme in the evangelism process of the early church is that of *church as mother*. The image of mother suggests that new Christians are not left on their own in a world of principalities and powers, but are brought into a community of people from whose bosom they are nourished and given all that is needed to survive.

Descriptions of the church as mother abound among the early church fathers. Tertullian speaks of "Our Lady Mother the Church"[23] who nourishes us "from her bountiful breasts."[24] Clement of Alexandria extols the church as "virgin and mother—pure as a virgin, loving as a mother."[25] Cyprian, whose writings on the church are replete with female imagery, proclaims the church to be "the one mother plentiful in the results of her fruitfulness: from her womb we are born, by her milk we are nourished, by her spirit we are animated."[26] But how does the church fulfill its mothering role? First, according to the early church fathers, the church is the womb in which God's children are born. This image of gestation appears as early as the second century in Justin Martyr's *First Apology*, a work written to the Emperor Titus to explain the Christian faith. Justin describes the church as a womb and draws an analogy between the water of baptism and the "moist seed" of conception. In the water of the church, the candidate is washed "in the name of God, Father and Lord of the universe, and of our Savior Jesus Christ, and of the Holy Spirit. . . . For Christ said, 'Except ye be born again, ye shall not enter into the kingdom of heaven.' "[27] Conversion to Christ takes place in the Church, in the water of its womb. In the waters of baptism, death to the old way of life and the resurrection to a new way of life are symbolized.[28]

The church is also mother because of the nurture it

provides. Augustine is so assured of the loving hand of the church that he can say, "You are safe, who have God for your Father and His Church for your mother."[29] In his treatise on baptism, Augustine stressed both the birthing and nurturing aspects of the church. The church "gives birth to all ... within her pale, of her own womb."[30] The church gives birth, nurses, cares for, and even agonizes over her children.

The third theological theme of evangelism in the early church is *evangelism as a process*. This assertion does not preclude the possibility of instant conversion. Certainly, there have been and will always be conversions "on the road to Damascus." But even these conversions require development and nurture. For example, Paul went away to Arabia, then, after three years, to Jerusalem for fifteen days to confer with Cephas. Next, he traveled to the regions of Syria and Cilicia. And finally, fourteen years after his conversion, he went to Jerusalem and on to his famous missionary work (Gal. 1:15–2:1). Exegetes agree that these fourteen years were a time of growth and development for Paul. Like Jesus, who "increased in wisdom and in stature, and in favor with God and man" (Luke 2:52 RSV), Paul underwent periods of growth. Consequently, the theology of evangelism in the early church looks upon salvation as a process that, even if preceded by a dramatic conversion, still requires a person to develop a responsible and dynamic relationship with Christ and the church through spiritual formation.

The notion of spiritual formation was not foreign to the early church fathers. Irenaeus, for example, states: "Man has first to come into being, then to progress, and by progressing come to manhood, and having reached manhood to increase, and thus increasing to persevere, and by persevering be glorified, and thus see his Lord." Irenaeus also argued that Christ himself sanctified the various stages of human life.[31] "He came to save all through his own person; all, that is, who through him are re-born to God; infants, children, boys, young men and old. Therefore he passed through every stage of life."[32] Today, the insights of Jean Piaget's cognitive developmental structuralism, Erik Erikson's psychological theory, and James Fowler's stages of spiritual growth provide a fertile contemporary basis for the restoration of an evangelism that takes into account various periods of development.

We see the concept of process in the worship, evangelism and nurture of the early church unfold through the four identifiable phases of development. The period of *seeker* presupposes an interest in the gospel. Next, the instruction of the *hearer* presupposes a strong degree of commitment. The period of the *kneeler* is a time of intense spiritual preparation for baptism. The final period of the *faithful* is full incorporation into the church.

The fourth theological theme deals with the *power of symbol*. Conversion and growth in Christ and the church are accomplished not only by words, but also by words made visible through performative symbol.[33] The principle of performative symbol is rooted in the Christian doctrine of incarnation. The confession that the human and divine are united in the person of Christ affirms that God can and does work through material and physical creation. God's saving presence is made a reality through physical signs. In the early church, the process of coming into Christ and his church is characterized not only by teaching but also by passage rites infused with participatory symbols. These visible words provide the convert with powerful life-changing symbols of their journey, and with memory markers that solidify their journey and bring, by way of recall in the worship life of the church, fresh experiences of the commitments they made to Christ in conversion. These passage rites include the conversion, covenant, and the powerful life-changing event of baptism.

Ancient evangelism occurred in a setting hostile to the church and its values; it developed in the context of a clear

self-understanding of the church as the eschatological people who are under the reign of God, the people who confess "Jesus is Lord." It was an evangelism with teeth, not an
"easy believism" or a "cheap grace"; and it was a spiritual
journey of discipleship, spiritual formation, and entrance
into a new community. We turn now to look at the situation
of the twenty-first century, a culture that bears similarity to
the pre-Constantinian times, and we ask: *How can we adapt
this kind of evangelism to our post-Christian world?*

3. The Missional Church Today

The condition of the present culture necessitates the recovery of the church's self-understanding as eschatological mission and calls for the recovery of the structure and principles of ancient evangelism. Therefore, I will

(1) *compare* our current cultural situation with that of the ancient pagan culture;
(2) *show* that the four theological themes of ancient evangelism have been recovered in today's world; and
(3) *suggest* we adapt the ancient process of evangelism in today's church.

The Cultural Situation of the Postmodern World

A common theme among present-day missiologists and theologians is the end of Christendom and the emergence of a postmodern world.

The end of the modern world and its particular way of thinking is captured by postmodern philosopher Jean-Francois Lyotard in *The Postmodern Condition*. He defines postmodernity as "incredulity toward meta narratives."[1] Lyotard, and all postmodern philosophers, argue that no single story provides a universally accepted understanding of the world. No one can agree on truth. Today's pluralistic world is characterized by numerous meta narratives, none of which can claim to provide universal truth for all. Pluralism and the failure to find universal truth has led us into total relativism. There is no unifying religion, no single worldview to give the world coherence and unity. Culture has been secularized and the end of Christendom has appeared. How did the secularization of the West and the arrival of the postmodern relativism occur?

The secularization of culture may be described as a movement away from historic religious sensibilities to a new condition of life. The "historic religious sensibilities" refer to the formation of Christendom after the conversion of Constantine, and especially to the christianization of Europe in the medieval era. This ideal of a christianized culture was maintained by the Reformers but gradually eroded during the last three centuries due to the rise of the Enlightenment, with its emphasis on the autonomy of the individual and the finality of reason. These views, coupled with the rise of science and technology, brought us to the new condition of life—secularism.[2]

Secularism is the widespread belief that the God of the Bible is irrelevant to everyday life. Modern thought has pushed God to the peripheral edge of life. The Christian God is not needed. Humanity has come of age and is no longer in need of Jesus Christ and the church. A way to imagine this shift in culture is to reflect on what stood at the center of life in the Middle Ages and what stands at the focal point of life today. During the Middle Ages the church stood at the center of life. In any city, town, or village the church building stood in the middle, with markets and houses forming a ring around the building and grounds. No matter where one was during the day—at home, at market, in the fields—the eyes could quickly fall on the church, the visual center of all of life. In today's world, the church is no longer at the center of life. Sociologists point to the mall with its consumerism or to the sports arena with its competition as focal points of interest. God has been removed from the center of life, and the church has been marginalized.[3]

In response to its marginalization, the church has tried to regain its status through inept means. The modern church has attempted to recover its place in society through the political agenda of Christendom. In recent decades, conservatives politicized the church by aligning itself with the Republican Party, while liberals politicized the church through the social agenda of the Democratic Party. Both appear to view the work of the church in society "to underwrite American democracy."[4] The church, having lost its distinct public face, has allowed itself to be reduced to the priestly ministry of overseeing culture and the caretaker of society. This denial of its true mission has resulted in a distinct confusion among the people of God. The attempt to realign itself with culture and emerge as a leader in politics has only resulted in the further demise and irrelevancy of the church. Consequently, the church in the West has lost its mission and is presiding over its own demise. The church must realize that accommodation to worldly political agendas is not the answer in a secular post-Christian society. Therefore it must find a new direction. Unfortunately, many pastors and congregations are still characterized by the Christendom understanding of the church. They continue to assume the role of chaplain to society or accommodate political agendas and cultural norms in the hope of reasserting the church's place of leadership in culture. This approach is hopeless and leads to endless frustration and even despair. So what should a congregation do?[5]

Recover the Eschatological Vision of the Church

First, a congregation needs to be awakened to the end of Christendom—it must stop viewing its function in society as chaplain and caretaker, and it needs to give up all pretenses to its favored status in society. The church is, as Hauerwas and Willimon note in *Resident Alien*, a stranger within the culture of the world. The church is in exile. Like the people of Israel, it is dominated by Egypt and exists as a sojourner in a strange and alien place. It has been carried into the desert, into the heart of the culture of death where it must find itself at the center of all that is alien to God, and there recover its identity.

Considering the situation of the church in this fallen culture, the second imperative for every congregation is to discover its true missional character. The church does not "have" a missionary program. It does not "send" missionaries out to other lands to proclaim the gospel. Instead, its true character is its embodiment of Christ's mission. By its very existence in the world, it witnesses to the mission of God *(Missio Dei)*, to the overthrow of evil and to the ultimate reign of God over the entire created order. This is the eschatological nature of the church. It is the presence of the future in a world hostile to its message and values (2 Pet. 3:10-18).

Missiologist and theologians have been rethinking the understanding of the church held during Christendom. Missiologists like Lesslie Newbigin[6] and David Bosch[7] have laid the groundwork for contemporary missiology. George Hunsberger and Craig Van Gelder in *The Church Between Gospel and Culture* have continued what Newbigin and Bosch began.[8] Hunsberger speaks of the current missiological issue as a "crisis touching the character of evangelism in a pluralistic, secularist setting" and suggests that "the crisis is first one of the identity of the church" that the postmodern world "cries out for a new . . . definition of the church itself."[9] He refers to Newbigin's understanding of the church as the "sign, instrument and foretaste" of the reign of God.[10] The church's mission in the world, then, is to represent the reign of God, to bring people under the present reign of God and to witness to the ultimate reign of God over the entire created order through worship and the ministries of the church. The church is an eschatological people, the hope of the world.

Stanley Hauerwas in *After Christendom?* reminds us that in pre-Constantinian days Christians recognized they were confronted by hostile powers, that they "knew those powers were already defeated," and this allowed them to make a "confident and joyful challenge to the pretentious power of Rome."[11] These Christians saw themselves as "participants in a grand drama of God's salvation of all creation." The church is, he states, "those gathered from the nations to testify to the resurrected Lord. Without the church the world literally has no hope of salvation since the church is necessary for the world to know it is part of a story that it cannot know without the church."[12] Many other voices have joined Hauerwas with a call to recover the true nature of the church as the people called to witness to the reign of God.

For example, evangelical Rodney Clapp echoes similar sentiments. He writes:

> Now that the long Constantinian age has all but passed, we Christians find ourselves in a situation much more closely analogous to that of New Testament Christians than to the Christendom for which some nostalgically long. The Bible, it turns out, offers abundant resources for living in a wildly diverse and contested world. With Constantine finally buried, theologians and biblical scholars find themselves able to reclaim, and present again to the church, the politics of Jesus.[13]

Hunsberger reminds us that "we are caught between a Constantinian Christendom that has ended and to which we cannot return and the culture's relegation of the church to the private realm, which is untenable if we rightly understand the gospel as news that is relevant to the public life of the whole world."[14]

The church, by restoring its eschatological self-understanding, not only has a story to tell but is itself the reality and embodiment of the story. It is the very presence of the *Missio Dei*. For "through the church, the manifold wisdom of God should be made known to the rulers and authorities in the heavenly realm" (Eph. 3:10). "The earliest Christian profession, 'Jesus is Lord,' was never merely a statement of personal devotion but a claim to universal validity. Christian mission made sense only on the premise that the crucified Jesus had been enthroned as the true Lord of the whole world, and thus claiming the allegiance of the whole world."[15]

This cosmic view of salvation is not only the view of the early church, but also the recovered view of missiologists and theologians of postmodernity. Their insights raise this question: Do we need to recover ancient evangelism in a world that has come to the end of Constantianism and is recovering its eschatological witness to a post-Christian world? If so, what does that evangelism look like?

The Message and Method of Evangelism in the Postmodern World

Hunsberger rightly recognizes that "the way in which we conceive evangelism needs an overhaul."[16] He suggests we need to rid ourselves of "our guilt-ridden motivational strategies."[17] The message of evangelism is "good news." It says the voluntary sacrifice of Jesus for sin was to pour out his life for others. Through the shedding of his blood new life was poured out to a world condemned because of the sin of the first Adam. Hence, the early church spoke of "the life-giving cross." By his sacrificial death, Christ destroyed death and conquered evil so that life might be restored to the whole world. When people are invited to "believe in Jesus," they are being called into his life and death, which is for both them and the world. It is a repentance from sin—going the wrong way under a slavery to evil—and an embracing of a new life under the reign of Christ in his body, the church. It is, as Paul said to the Romans, a burial into his death so that "we should no longer be slaves to sin," and a union with his resurrection so that we may be "alive to God in Christ Jesus" (Rom. 6:1-14 NIV).[18] Peter refers to the impact of the eschatological vision: "Since everything will be destroyed (that is, all powers of evil) . . . , what kind of people ought you to be? You ought to live holy and godly lives" (2 Pet. 3:11). This message is expressed by Justin Martyr, who made note of people turning their backs on "violence and tyranny" because they saw how Christians were "free of the addictions of greed, sex, xenophobia and the bondage of the magic arts."[19] Evangelism in the postmodern world is a turning away from evil to enter a community where there is a *"Credible Demonstration* that life lived by the pattern of commitment to Jesus is imaginable, possible, and relevant."[20]

The witness of the Christian faith in the postmodern world is not rational argument and, in the words of Josh McDowell, "evidence that demands a verdict," but lives that have been changed and communities that have been transformed by God's presence among them. In a transformed community, Christians will not quarrel among themselves but will be anxious to listen to, respect, and love one another. This may seem like a lofty ideal, but it is possible. In vital churches, people are committed to communicate with one another through the language of love. In a postmodern world, confrontations such as "you're wrong and here's why" do not communicate. Only when people are approached through love and acceptance will we "have gained the opportunity and freedom to influence."[21] For this reason the postmodern church needs to be characterized by "humility."[22] Humility is a quiet, patient evangelism that not only "tells" the way but "shows" the way. The evangelizing community of faith is an inviting and compelling community of people who attract the unchurched because they embody the new life under the reign of Christ informed by their eschatological vision. The message of evangelism is that the whole world will come under his reign, but the *method* of evangelism is to bring people one by one under the reign of God through a journey of making Jesus Christ their personal Lord and Savior. For while Jesus is "for the whole world," he is also "for me." Our personal journey into Christ therefore is nourished by the community called "church," which God has set as a divine presence to proclaim the ultimate destiny of the world. Without the church the world has no idea of its destiny. How do we bring people into Christ and the church in a postmodern world? Through an adaptation of the ancient evangelism the postmodern church can present a process in which a real personal and life-changing commitment is made to Jesus Christ. This evangelism is possible because the substance of the ancient model and the four theological convictions—*Christus Victor; the church as mother; evangelism as process;* and *performative symbol*—have all been recovered in recent theological thinking. Since these themes will be developed at greater length in the adaptation of the ancient model, a brief presentation of their restoration is sufficient at this point.

Following World War II, Gustaf Aulén resurrected the term *Christus Victor* in his book by the same name. Aulén says, "The main idea is clear. The work of Christ is first and foremost a victory over the powers which hold 'mankind' in bondage: sin, death, and the devil."[23] His work has been followed by the three-volume study of Walter Wink, *Naming the Powers, Unmasking the Powers,* and *Engaging the Powers.* Add to this the work of Hendrik Berkhof, *Christ and the Powers,* and Gregory Boyd's *God at War.* The *Christus Victor* is central to the missiological writings of postmodernity and to all current discussions of spiritual warfare.[24]

Second, the new studies on the church point to the resurgence of the *church as mother.* There is a recovered emphasis on the church as a nurturing and caring community. Carl Braaten in *Mother Church* approvingly quotes Augustine: "Behold the womb of Mother Church: see how she groans and is in travail to bring you forth and guide you on into the light of faith."[25] Craig Van Gelder, in *The*

Essence of the Church, writes: "When we encounter the church, we move into spiritual territory that occupies earthly terrain. We encounter the living God in the midst of our humanity. We encounter the Spirit of God dwelling in the midst of a people who are created and formed into a unique community."[26] In and through this community the converting person is nurtured, discipled, and equipped.

There is also a recovery of *evangelism as process.* Recent studies in education recognize that people who are incorporated into the church must go through a process. The most noted proponent of process is James Fowler, *The Stages of Faith* and *Becoming Adult, Becoming Christian.*[27] Fowler says, "One of the principal reasons for the present widespread acceptance and embrace of psychological theories of adult development . . . is that they provide us with narrative frameworks for holding together our profound experiences of change and continuity . . . and powerfully speak to the situation of cultural ferment and confusion . . . in our society today."[28] He and others, like Thomas Groome *(Christian Religious Education)* and Parker Palmer *(To Know As We Are Known),* understand the power of story in the process of spiritual formation and growth.[29]

Finally, recent studies in communication theory point to the *power of symbol.* Symbols are the "language of the supernatural." They deal with "intuition, with imagination, and with emotion rather than with thinking, sensations, or the will."[30] For Tom Driver, rituals "not only reflect the way the world is ordered, but actually serve to put . . . order in place."[31] This image speaks powerfully to the rituals and symbols of the evangelism process, both old and new. Evangelism is in a very real sense a reordering of one's world. To come into Christ and the church is to come into a new way of seeing.

I began this section with a reference to my experience at St. Mark's in Philadelphia. My concern is for St. Mark's and other traditional churches that are asking how to do evangelism in a postmodern pluralistic world. Should we give up and hope for a trickle of people to find us? Should we do a mass evangelism as in a Billy Graham crusade? Should we take a traditional church and shape it into a seeker church?

Now, for the first time in centuries, the church has been freed from the Constantinian model. The end of Christendom and the emergence of a neo-pagan culture bring us full circle to a society similar to premodern times. In this situation the goal of the church is to recover its eschatological witness and be the embodied future-present community that can invite people to come into its sphere and find new life. This is evangelism of a new sort. It is, as Lesslie Newbigin wrote, "being turned round in order to recognize and participate in the dawning reality of God's reign. But this inward turning immediately and intrinsically involves both a pattern of conduct and a visible companionship. It involves membership in a community and a decision to act in certain ways."[32]

Here are some steps to help you become an evangelizing church in today's culture:

1. Do all you can to understand the pagan nature of this culture. Talk to your teenagers and young people. Read the "signs of the times" in the media. Listen to the text of culture.
2. Restore the following theological themes:
   - *Christus Victor*
   - *church as mother*
   - *evangelism as process*
   - *performative power of symbol*

We turn now to examine more closely how this ancient practice of evangelism can be adapted to transform the lives of not only individuals, but also that of the entire church, making it an effective witness in today's world.

Leader's Guide

A. EVALUATE THE EFFECTIVENESS OF YOUR CHURCH IN THESE FOUR AREAS
- Is Christ presented as victor over the powers of evil in our lives? In the world?
- Does this congregation nurture new Christians?
- How can we make our evangelism more a process of conversion *and* spiritual formation?
- Do we use symbolism effectively so as to provide converting people and believers spiritual experiences to remember and reflect upon?

B. PLANNING A COURSE OF ACTION TO REVITALIZE THE CONGREGATION

Invite a group of teenagers and twenty-somethings from your church to form a "focus group." Ask, "What's going on in your world?" Listen. Probe. Be open. Ask yourself the following: How well does this church relate the gospel to this culture? What do we need to learn? How do we need to change? Are we ready for outreach?

C. PLANNING A COURSE OF ACTION FOR OUTREACH

Do the same as above:
- How do we reach out?
- Who will be involved?
- When and how should we start?

Resources for Further Reading

Your reading should concentrate on the themes of *Christus Victor*, mother church, process evangelism, and the power of symbol. I suggest Gustaf Aulén, *Christus Victor* (New York: Macmillan, 1986), which is out of print but worth the effort to find through inter-library loan; Rodney Clapp, *A Peculiar People* (Downers Grove, Ill.: InterVarsity Press, 1996); James W. Fowler, *Becoming Adult, Becoming Christian* (San Francisco: Jossey-Bass, 2000); Aidan Nichols, *The Art of God Incarnate* (Grand Rapids, Eerdmans, 1980).

II

Evangelizing the Seeker

REACHING THE UNCHURCHED

JOURNEY TO JESUS

SEEKER

Spiritual Goal:
   Conversion
Passage Rite:
   Rite of
   Conversion
Resource:
   Follow Me!

INTRODUCTION

My father was a pastor of Montgomeryville Baptist Church, located about twenty-five miles west of Philadelphia. The church dates back to the 1700s; tradition holds that George Washington once worshiped there. Whether the legend is true or not, it is indeed an old church surrounded by a large cemetery, where the tombstones of Native Americans and many other people date as far back as the early seventeenth century.

My pre-evangelism began during my adolescence, when I read the epitaphs of people whose enduring testimonies were inscribed on roughly hewn tombstones in the cemetery. I suspect that I always believed the faith, having grown up in an atmosphere of belief in God and trust in Christ. But my spiritual sensibilities were jarred, even more fully awakened, when I was thirteen and my father said, "Robert, don't you think it's time you became baptized?" For reasons that I could not then give, the image of baptism forced me to inquire more deeply within myself to determine whether my intentions of faith were strong enough to allow for a step as decisive as entrance into the waters of baptism. My father's question was not a matter of simple cognitive faith, but a call to take up the cross and make a lifelong commitment to follow Jesus.

My experience illustrates the meaning of seeker time. For the congregation it is evangelism time. For the seeker it is a time to make a commitment, to set one's face in the direction of baptism. This section explores seeker evangelism in the early church (ch. 4), translates these principles to evangelism today (ch. 5), and finally describes the rite of conversion (ch. 6), the passage rite that opens the seeker's path toward baptism.

4. Evangelism in the Ancient World

The two most important questions to ask about evangelism in the ancient church are

(1) *What* was the message of early Christians?
(2) *How* was this message communicated?

To answer these questions, let's turn first to theological studies on evangelism in the early church, and second to sociological research on early church growth. These studies will help us understand why Christianity was so effective against paganism in the first three centuries, and stimulate our thinking for evangelism today.

The Early Christian Message

Michael Green summarizes the message of the early church as "nothing less than the joyful announcement of the long awaited Messianic salvation, when God had come to the rescue of a world in need";[1] . . . "the early preachers of the good news had one subject and one only, Jesus";[2] . . . "the one who came preaching the good news has become the content of the good news";[3] . . . "the earliest Christians regarded Jesus . . . as embodying in his person and achievement the kingly rule of God himself";[4] . . . "intended for the whole world . . . the gospel of God's kingly rule proclaimed to the Jews is meant for the Gentiles too";[5] . . . "it embraces rescue from sin and death as well as political liberation";[6] . . . "[Christ as] ruler sits on the throne of the universe";[7] . . . "[this] Christian evangel came like a spark to the tinder of ancient society";[8] . . . "the announcement of the climax of history, the divine intervention . . .

brought about by the incarnation, life, death, resurrection and heavenly session of Jesus of Nazareth";[9] . . . "a victory over hostile forces."[10]

This message of *Missio Dei* originated with Jesus and the apostles. The initial message of Jesus was simply "follow me." As the disciples and others gathered around him they learned more and more about the content of their commitment. They learned that Jesus had entered into the strong man's house and bound him. And, because this was true, the kingdom of God had arrived among them (Matt. 12:1-12). The apostle John seems to be particularly fascinated by the image that Jesus has overcome the evil one. In his Gospel there are numerous references to the overthrow of the kingdom of evil, and the inauguration of the rule of God over all things through Jesus Christ. He quotes the words of Jesus: "The prince of this world now stands condemned" (John 16:11 NIV); "Take heart! I have overcome the world" (John 16:33 NIV); and "Now is the time for judgment on this world; now the prince of this world will be driven out" (John 12:30 NIV).

This message of the victory of God's mission to the world was articulated on the day of Pentecost. Peter proclaimed the meaning of the life, death, and resurrection of Christ and concluded his sermon with the words: "Let all the house of Israel therefore know assuredly that God has made him both Lord and Christ, this Jesus whom you crucified" (Acts 2:36 RSV). Luke described the result: "When they heard this they were cut to the heart" (Acts 2:37 RSV). The message had hit home, it penetrated into their hearts and created *seeking*. "Brethren, what shall we do?" To which Peter responded, "Repent, and be baptized every one of you in the name of Jesus Christ for the forgiveness of your sins" (Acts 2:37-38 RSV). In this Pentecost narrative we see a twofold movement: the first step proclaims the gospel and awakens faith. It cuts "to the heart" and prompts the seeker to ask "What shall I do?" When the seeker comes to faith, the second step begins—the journey to baptism and a life under the reign of Christ.

How Was the Message Communicated?

The gospel was communicated through synagogues, open-air preaching, personal testimony, home evangelism, worship, literature, and the impact of Christian commitment to societal need and personal encounters.[11] These are the methods. But the question is how. "How did a tiny and obscure messianic movement from the edge of the Roman Empire dislodge classical paganism and become the dominant faith of Western civilization?"[12] Sociologist Rodney Stark answers this question in *The Rise of Christianity*. Stark's study says something of what the church should look like today.

Christian faith was spread through *pre-existing social networks*. According to Stark, these networks included one-on-one contacts that Christians had in their homes, among neighbors and friends, at places of work, and through extended travel and commerce.[13] New Christians whose lives had been transformed by the gospel immediately told and won their innermost circle of family and friends. Personal contact was the key.

But Christianity also spread through the impact of the church as the witness to God's mission (Eph. 3:10). First, the church spread because it became known for its *compassion*. For example, during the third and fourth centuries, devastating deadly epidemics occurred in which numerous people died. The pagans fled and cared only for themselves. But the Christians reached out in loving help to care for the sick and the needy.[14] Stark summarizes the impact of the compassionate church:

> Christianity . . . arose in response to the misery, chaos, fear, and brutality of life in the urban Greco-Roman world. . . . To cities filled with the homeless and impov-

erished, Christianity offered charity as well as hope. To cities filled with newcomers and strangers, Christianity offered an immediate basis for attachments. To cities filled with orphans and widows, Christianity provided a new and expanded sense of family. To cities torn by violent ethnic strife, Christianity offered a new basis for social solidarity. . . . And to cities faced with epidemics, fires, and earthquakes, Christianity offered effective nursing services.[15]

Because of its service to those in need, ancient local churches "gained a reputation" for their faith and unselfish giving to others. They stood in the tradition of the church at Ephesus, of whom Paul said: "I heard about your faith in the Lord Jesus and your love for all the saints" (Eph. 1:15 NIV). The church that is "heard" for its good deeds and love will always draw people who are in need and searching for hope.

Second, Christianity spread because of its commitment to the *sanctity of life*. In the Roman world, abortion and infanticide were common. "Abortion," states Stark, "not only prevented many births, it killed many women . . . , and it resulted in a substantial incidence of infertility in women who survived abortions."[16] The Roman family, due to abortions and infanticide (especially of female babies) remained small, and "men greatly outnumbered women."[17] For example, "a study of inscriptions at Delphi made it possible to reconstruct six hundred families. Of these, only six had raised more than one daughter."[18] Because Christian families loved and nourished their female babies and also took in female babies who had been abandoned by pagan families, the church grew. "Christianity" writes Stark, "was unusually appealing because within the Christian subculture women enjoyed far higher status than did women in the Greco-Roman world."[19] The early church practiced the teaching of Paul: "There is neither Jew nor Greek, slave nor free, male nor female, for you are all one in Christ Jesus" (Gal. 3:28 NIV). The church that has high regard for life, women, minorities, and those who suffer "draws" the seeker because the seeker sees an authentic Christianity.

Next, Christianity spread rapidly because of the *high level of commitment* expected of new Christians. Stark writes "commitment is energy"[20] and reminds us "when commitment levels are high, groups can undertake all manner of collective actions."[21] Seekers wanted the discipline and the guidance of the evangelism process. Christians did not find commitment to be binding; rather, commitment freed them to become more fully human and experience what Paul taught: "It is for freedom that Christ has set us free" (Gal. 5:1 NIV).

Finally, Christianity spread because of the *communal factor*. It fulfilled the need to belong. Christians were not an aggregate of individuals, but a community characterized by a communal spirit, a common life, and a common vision. E. R. Dodds, in *Pagan and Christian in an Age of Anxiety*, points to the common life of the church as a reason for its success over paganism:

> A Christian congregation was from the first a community in a much fuller sense than any corresponding group of Isiac or Mithraist devotees. Its members were bound together not only by common rites but by a common way of life. . . . Love of one's neighbour is not an exclusively Christian virtue, but in [this] period Christians appear to have practised it much more effectively than any other group. The Church provided the essentials of social security. . . . But even more important, I suspect, than these material benefits was the sense of belonging which the Christian community could give.[22]

Dodds summarizes the keys to an effective evangelism: *community, common rites, a common way of life, love of neighbor, security, sense of belonging*. The ancient church attracted people because it spoke to their spiritual needs. Consider this: If it is true that we have been created for life with God, then it is also true that our life in the family of Father, Son, and Holy Spirit is communal. The church is the beginning of that communal life in the here and now. The congregation that understands the theology of community will commit to being the community of God's dwelling on earth, and thus will "draw" others.

In sum, the early church evangelized the Roman Empire and overcame paganism because of the personal witness of individual Christians and because of the corporate witness of the congregations whose inner life and outer actions demonstrated the continuing presence of Jesus Christ in and to the world. The church was, as we have seen by its very existence in society, mission. This is the missional church.

But how did the church communicate Christ to the seeker and engender such commitment? It was through the sevenfold process of evangelism which began with the first step—"Follow me." We turn now to examine what the ancient church meant by the call to follow Jesus. Through this study we will gain insight on the "how" of evangelism in today's post-Christian world.

Follow Me

The initial step of salvation is found in the words of Jesus—"Follow me." But why the process? Why the journey? Why four stages and three passages rites? *The process was developed for the conversion of pagans.* The first Christians were Jews who had the moral training of their Hebrew background. They were baptized immediately (Acts 2:37-41). However, because the message of the church was also heard by pagans with no training in character and values, and no understanding of God's work in history with Israel, the church developed an extensive form of discipleship and spiritual formation. The church needed to wean pagan converts from their immoral way of life, from their allegiance to Caesar, from their belief in many gods, and from their faith in magic, the occult, and astrology.[23] Because they were ignorant of Christian faith and practice, pagans needed time to develop their understanding of what it meant to be a Christian and a member of the church.

Those who are to be baptized into Jesus' death had to learn to "walk in newness of life" (Rom. 6:4). Baptism signifies that "our old self was crucified with him so that the body of sin might be destroyed, and we might no longer be enslaved to sin" (Rom. 6:7). The message was quite simple: *Turn away from your commitment to the gods of this world and live a new life in Jesus with the community of the church.* Faith in Christ was political, ethical, and communal. Living under the reign of God meant a new political allegiance, a new set of ethical values, and a communal life among the people of God. These values had to be learned.[24]

In the previous chapter, I indicated that converting persons were expected to turn away from all allegiances to the gods of this world, refuse to work in any occupation that required an allegiance to Caesar, and turn away from occupations that were immoral. Ethical instructions admonished seekers not only to "turn away" from evil but also to turn *toward* a new life.

> If a man has a wife or a woman a husband, let the man be instructed to content himself with his wife and the woman to content herself with her husband. But if a man is unmarried, let him be instructed to abstain from impurity, either by lawfully marrying a wife or else by remaining as he is.[25]

Seekers were also called to turn away from any reliance on astrology and false religions: "An enchanter, an astrologer, a diviner, a soothsayer, a user of magic verses, a juggler, a mounteband, an amulet maker must desist or be rejected."[26]

The spirit in these instructions was the matter of allegiance and style. The choice to come under the reign of God in Jesus Christ means a shift of commitment. The seeker is taught there is a war going on between the reality of evil that is destructive and binding and the reality of God that frees us from the binding power of evil. Seeker witness always presents the message that "he has rescued us from the dominion of darkness and brought us into the kingdom of the Son . . . in whom we have redemption" (Col. 1:13-14 NIV). And this is made possible because Jesus "having disarmed the powers and authorities . . . made a public spectacle of them, triumphing over them by the cross" (Col. 2:15 NIV). Therefore, the seeker is to repent *(metanoia)* from the old way of life and turn to the new way of life under the reign of God. This kind of conversion is not an instant accomplishment done in the secret chambers of the heart, but a lifelong public commitment, a process that responds to the call of Jesus Christ to "follow me" by repenting from an old way of life and setting one's journey toward a new life symbolized in baptism into Jesus Christ—a drowning to all that is sin and death, and a resurrection to a new life under the reign of Christ.

Chapter 5 demonstrates how these principles of ancient evangelism—the message, the missional nature of the church, and the call to "follow me" (the first of the four phases)—are all transferable to the evangelism of the local church in today's world.

5. Evangelism Today

In the first section I argued that the cultural situation of today's church is neo-pagan and much like that of the Roman Empire. Consequently, we need to recover the message and method of an evangelism that was effective within the paganism of the Roman world. From the early church we gain five insights into this evangelism: the need to

(1) have a *missional self-understanding*
(2) recognize that *evangelism requires a renewed congregation*
(3) call individuals to *commit to their social networks*
(4) establish a *"reputation for servanthood"*
(5) establish the *process for the formation of new Christians*

The Evangelizing Church Needs to Have a Missional Self-understanding

The first question a local congregation must ask is, Do we understand what it means to be *the missional church?*[1] The true church is not an institution governed by secular principles of business or social management. The social sciences may serve the human side of managing the facilities and budgets of the church, but they cannot define the purpose and goal of the church—to signify and represent the mission of God. The healthy church understands itself as the presence of Christ in the world with a mission to embody, proclaim, and enact the salvation of the world through the *Missio Dei* accomplished and inaugurated by the life and ministry of Jesus and completed in the eschaton. Such a church acts as a communal witness to the overthrow of the powers of evil and to the reign of God over all creation (Ephesians). This kind of healthy, vibrant, theologically self-understood church is not an option but a necessary requirement for the church that would be a worshiping, evangelizing, and nurturing community. Recent studies on the theology of the church show that healthy churches are moving away from the management and CEO models of the 1970s and 1980s toward the recovery of a more authentic biblical self-understanding. Eddie Gibbs, in *ChurchNext: Quantum Changes in How We Do Ministry*,[2] writes out of an understanding of postmodern culture and calls the church to recognize "a missionary challenge that is more urgent and radical than it has been for many generations."[3] He suggests "the most helpful models might be drawn from the first 150 years of the Christian church."[4] Therefore he calls on the church to stop living in the past (modernity) and to engage with the present (postmodernity); to move away from the market-driven approach to a mission-driven view of the church; to get past the bureaucratic hierarchies characterized by powers and move toward apostolic models of servant leadership; to bring an end to preparing ministers as professionals and develop true servant leadership; to break with the current fascination with celebrities and recover spiritual formation by exposure to the saints of the church; to break with the maintenance of a dead orthodoxy to recover the vitality of a living faith; and to be less concerned with numbers and crowds so that an authentic attempt to reach the unchurched will be set in motion.[5]

These themes are also expressed in the work of Inagrace Dietterich and her Chicago-based Center for Parish Development. At the heart of Dietterich's work is a call to recover an ecclesiology driven primarily by theological considerations, with a secondary emphasis on the management sciences. The people of God are called, she writes, "to be *faithful*: to discern, interpret, and proclaim the gospel of Jesus Christ. . . . And they are also called to be *effective*: to structure and manage themselves in such a way that they practice efficient stewardship of all available resources (i.e., human, financial, program, and facilities)."[6]

Dietterich is concerned about the dualisms we create when we don't function out of the biblical and theological model of the church as the Body of Christ. Dietterich's research and experience show that a theological understanding of the church which regards faith as only an individual matter disregards the communal nature of faith. It supports the privatization of faith and fails to focus on the living experience of embodied faith in a Christian people who shape a communal spirituality. As a result, the church is seen as a mere human or social institution that is governed best by the social sciences. This desupernaturalized view of the church undermines the true spiritual reality of the community of God's people on earth and renders it ineffective as the context in which evangelism and nurture occur. Do you want to be an evangelizing church in the postmodern world? Start here. Understand and put into practice what it means to be a missional church.

Evangelism Proceeds from a Renewed Congregation

Second, if we want to be a missional church we must be a *renewed church*. When I first became interested in the process of evangelism of the early church several years ago, I learned of a church that had put the ancient principles into practice. I called and made an appointment to interview the director, who made a comment that I will never forget. "We began this process," she said "without paying attention to the inner life of the church. We soon discovered it is not possible to bring new life into a dead church. New Christians will not survive. Consequently, we stopped the outreach process and paid attention to the renewal of the congregation. Once we became renewed and achieved the vitality of an alive congregation of faith, we were ready to return to seeker outreach."

I didn't know it at the time, but her comment introduced me to the postmodern way of evangelism. In the old way of witness, we asked the unchurched to believe in Christ, then to come to the church. In the postmodern form of witness we bring people to Christ through the church. The church is the doorway to Christ. For this reason, if we are to be an evangelizing church in today's world, we must begin with a healthy, vital body of believing, worshiping, discipling, nurturing, and socially active people—a church that is the continuation of the incarnate presence of Jesus in the world—a communal embodiment of what is preached.

For example, a young woman told me she had been a nihilist in college and rejected the possibility of any supernatural reality. However, as this view of life grew thin, she found herself affirming New Age spirituality. Because of her new spirituality, a friend invited her to church. Her friend spoke positively about this church, so she wanted to attend. The young woman found the atmosphere prayerful, congenial to discussion, and embracing. She felt warmly received and accepted without pressure. She eventually became involved with the people of the church on a personal level and joined a Bible study group and prayer fellowship. In none of these situations did anybody sit her down and confront her New Age views. Instead, she said, "As I was exposed to the people and to the Scriptures I gradually became christianized. One day it dawned on me how far I had come from my initial New Age viewpoint to an affirmation of a thoroughly biblical and Christian embracing of faith." This is postmodern evangelism—process in a relational and communal atmosphere of embodied faith, an awakening of faith in a healthy community of believers.

Research done by the Alban Institute confirms the claim that evangelism begins with a healthy church. Their study of growing congregations shows that people are not necessarily attracted to the church because of an "formal assimilation process," but because the church exudes a "positive personality"[7] demonstrated through its inner energy, practice of inclusion, and a sense of unique identity. Consultants found that in energetic and vital churches "people were there throughout the week and they were involved in something—running the church, cleaning it up, studying the Bible, praying, helping others."[8] These vital churches practiced inclusion. "They saw themselves as friendly, open, interested in newcomers, wanting others to be included in what they were doing and to share in the excitement of being a member of this religious community."[9] These vital churches are also characterized by a specific identity. They think of themselves as "special, unique, not like anyone else." They have a "message" that forms "community" and results in a "revitalizing spirit that [extends] throughout the membership."[10]

I travel a great deal and visit many churches. In some I feel a deadness. The people file in without much conversation. The worship is listless, boring, and uninspiring or a performance that seeks to entertain me. The people leave. No one speaks to me. I'm glad to leave. I vow, "I'll never go back there again." But then again I visit churches that are full of life. For example, in a recent visit to a midwestern Baptist church, I stood in the foyer, waiting for a friend, and I watched as the people poured in. It was raining hard, but there was no dampening of the spirit. The people acted as if they *wanted* to be in church. The church had an atmosphere of warmth and an excitement that was catching. I watched people greet one another and stand in small circles talking and laughing together. Several people walked up to me and asked, "Can I help you?" I consequently thought, "This is powerful. This church is so inviting." How do you create this kind of environment? The answer is *hospitality*.

Recent literature shows a resurgence of the place of hospitality in evangelism. In a remarkably helpful book

Making Room: Recovering Hospitality as a Christian Tradition, the author Christine Pohl speaks of hospitality as "a way of life fundamental to Christian identity"[11] and recounts her earliest experience of hospitality at the Community Bible Church in metropolitan New York. This church, she writes,

> had a heart so big that it welcomed hundreds of refugees, local poor people, and troubled souls. It was multiethnic before that was popular, and it introduced ordinary New Yorkers to the joy of hearing a hymn sung in four or five languages simultaneously. It was there I learned to cherish potluck dinners where you were never entirely sure what you were eating but it usually tasted good, and the fellowship tasted a bit like the kingdom. At CBC I discovered that hospitality to strangers required a sense of humor—especially the capacity to laugh at ourselves, to trust God to rescue us and others from the unintended consequences of our good efforts, and to continue on when we realized we'd been used.[12]

The hospitable community is a kind of "cultural transmission evangelism" as opposed to the more confrontational approach of modernity. Like the evangelism of Jesus, the church invites people into community so that they can "see" and "experience" a people radically committed to living out the principles of the Kingdom. This is a community not only open to others, but one committed to be a witness. As the seeker becomes associated with this kind of community, the commitment is caught, and, like those around them, the seekers gradually assume the communal character of faith and the commitment it demands.[13]

Postmodernity is marked by a longing for this kind of community. The disintegration of life has resulted in the loss of an integrating center. The church was once the center of life, but as Christianity became increasingly privatized, the family emerged as the central organizing principle of life, and now the breakdown of the family has resulted in the rise of the individual as the autonomous center of life. For example, a *Newsweek* article comments that today's teens spend more time with their peers than with their parents.[14] This "latch-key generation" longs for community and a sense of belonging. The Christian understanding of life claims that we are made in the image of the Triune God who lives in the community of Father, Son, and Holy Spirit, and because of that reality we are incomplete without community. The church is not to be a mere ordinary community, but one of a special sort because it is God's second act of creation, that foretaste of the kingdom to come. Entrance into a warm, loving, growing, and caring community is already an entrance into Christ, because it is a participation in the atmosphere of his body, in the reality of faith. As Jean Vanier, points out "There is a new realization that community is the place of meeting with God."[15] Want to be an evangelizing church in a postmodern world? Create a lively, energetic, enthusiastic, inclusive community.

Evangelism Results from Individual Witness in Social Networks

The third prerequisite for evangelism in a post-Christian world is a local church that is characterized by love, openness, inclusion, enthusiasm, and a sense of servanthood, and is ready to receive newcomers and journey them into faith. The next question is, How does this kind of church make contact with the unchurched?

Members of the church must exhibit an enthusiastic willingness to *tell other people in their immediate social networks* about the church and its people. This has been called "gossip-evangelism." For example, a woman who recently came back to the faith told me, "I'm absolutely in love with my church. I tell everyone about my church. When I encounter people with out-of-control lives, broken hearts and marriages, confused and lonely spirits, I don't say, 'Here are four things you need to believe.' I say, 'I have found the most wonderful, loving, embracing community in the world. My life has been completely changed. Come with me and see for yourself.' " I said to her, "You sound like an evangelist." She smiled and said, "Yep, I guess I am."

This woman's testimony provides us with a clear example of individual postmodern witness. It is not the confrontational witness that many people find uncomfortable and are reluctant to engage in. Let me give you an example.

I was a "preacher boy" at Bob Jones University in Greenville, South Carolina, in the 1950s. Bob Jones Sr. was an evangelist in the early decades of the twentieth century and founded the university to keep the fires of evangelism burning. During my student days he taught the "preacher boy" class, which consisted of approximately one thousand students who were planning to go into ministry. The major requirement was for each student to witness to seven people a week. For me, this assignment resulted in a "hit-and-run evangelism." Because I was busy with studies and campus activities, my fulfillment of the required seven witnesses (which had to be written and turned in weekly) was a quick Saturday afternoon trip to Greenville where I would hand out tracts on the street corner, at a gas station, at a restaurant, in a pharmacy or clothing store, or anywhere I could catch someone's attention for a moment or more. Needless to say, my witness was quite ineffective and probably did little more than meet the legal requirement of seven contacts per week. It was also an evangelism done out of "duty" and driven by guilt. I never enjoyed doing it, was always embarrassed by my own method, and felt that my witness was based on technique. In other words, my evangelism was not genuine and I ended up feeling like a phony.

The kind of evangelism developed by the early church does not push people. It is not individualistic nor based on immediacy. It is not technique or manipulation. It does not arise out of guilt. It does not embarrass. It does not put the unchurched person "on the spot."

Missional evangelism is indirect, authentic, and real. It arises out of relationship in the family, the neighborhood, the workplace and social situations. It does not depend totally upon the person giving witness. It connects with the support system provided by the community that lives under the reign of God. The Christian brings the unchurched to a healthy vibrant community of faith and, through association with an embodied community, faith is discussed and caught as the gospel is overheard.

This form of personal contact is the primary means of bringing people to Christ and the church. For example, according to the research of the American Growth Institute, people who come to church come because they have been influenced to do so by

Friend or relative	79%
Pastor	6%
Sunday school	5%
Walk-in	3%
Program	3%
Special Need	2%
Visitation	1%
Evangelism Crusade	.5%[16]

Clearly, the statistics show that personal contact within social networks is the point of most fruitful contact. The next, and ultimately the most crucial, part of the process is to bring the seeker into the community where living under the reign of Christ is demonstrated. Coming to church may start with a men's breakfast, a women's tea, a home Bible study fellowship, an Alcoholics Anonymous meeting, or some other group designed to touch people where they hurt or struggle. As the interests of the seeker grows, the seeker is invited to Sunday worship and follow-up discussion either one-on-one or in a small group in a home, a restaurant, or some other comfortable meeting place. If the discussion is in a small group, the group may bear a simple name such as "seekers" fellowship. Its mission can be expressed as "a time of inquiry for all who want to know what it means to follow Jesus." This time needs to be informal, open-ended, and without pressure. The goal is to discuss the Christian faith and allow the Holy Spirit to work in the heart and mind of the seeker.

To facilitate this kind of discussion, the Institute for Worship Studies has prepared a small booklet entitled *Follow Me!*[17] Its purpose is to enter into dialogue with the seeker as Jesus did with Cleopas on the road to Emmaus (Luke 24). It contains Scripture passages that present the message of Jesus, and questions for thought and discussion. The person witnessing may say, "Here's a little book that will give you some more information on what it means to follow Jesus. Why don't you read it and let's talk about it." The combination of a personal friend or small group, plus Scriptures to read and reflect upon with a loving, caring, energetic community of people who live out the faith is a womb-like atmosphere where the conception of faith may take place.

For example, a friend conducted a Bible study in his home. One of his unchurched neighbors attended regularly and engaged intently in the discussions. But he always came back to one issue: "I can't believe in that virgin birth idea." My friend handled the matter with great skill by saying, "Don't worry about the virgin birth. The real issue is not the virgin birth but your need to have Jesus. When Jesus is in your life the question of the virgin birth will take care of itself." One night my friend received a call from his neighbor saying, "I've got to see you right away; I need Jesus. I still don't know what to do about that virgin birth teaching, but right now I don't care. I just know that I need Jesus." This man came to Jesus, and sure enough, my friend was right—the matter of the virgin birth fell into place as a confession of faith.

The point is that people are converted not because they

have been given answers, but because they have experienced the embracing love of a community. I saw this back in the 1970s. Some of my students who had lost faith were sent by their parents to study under Francis Schaeffer at L'Abri Fellowship in Switzerland. Schaeffer was the intellectual guru of the students affected by nihilism and he was very persuasive, but always in a loving and compassionate way. When the students returned to college with restored faith, I always made it a point to ask, "So what brought you back to faith?" I was looking for the key intellectual argument, the idea that brought them to their knees, the thought that captured their imagination and drove them back to Jesus. The answer was always the same, "Well, it really wasn't Schaeffer's intellectual arguments, as good as they were, it was the love of the community. I've never experienced anything like it." This is postmodern evangelism.

Evangelism Will Result from a Church with a "Reputation"

In the previous chapter, we saw how the early church made an impact on society by serving its needs in the time of epidemics and other "crises." According to Rodney Stark, "Christianity revitalized life in Greco-Roman cities by providing new norms and new kinds of social relationships able to cope with many urgent urban problems."[18] I have observed, and I'm sure you have too, that growing congregations are "giving" congregations. They give away their space and time. They organize small groups to help the handicapped, single mothers, people bound by addictions, establish recovery groups, and the like. In this way they are always "reaching out" and "offering a helping hand" and demonstrating the servanthood ministry to which they have been called as a missional church. A church wishing to be an evangelizing community must create a reputation.

Grace Episcopal Church has a reputation in

Jacksonville, Florida. This church is the campus for one of the Institute for Worship Studies graduate programs. It's a "giving" community. For example, this church has hardly enough space for its own ministries but is still giving space away to groups not even associated with the church, groups doing works of mercy and charity for the community. Walk on that campus any time during the day or evening and it's full of people, energy, and excitement. The people are warm, friendly, outgoing and inclusive. Three Sunday services are full. Worship is powerful, moving, participatory, enthusiastic, and healing. The congregation sings heartily, laughs a lot and exudes the spirit of community. This is a church you "hear about," a church where "you've got to go there and see what's happening." There are many churches like Grace in every denomination and fellowship; and they are evangelizing, spiritually healthy, vital, and energetic communities of faith and relationship. "We found," Oswald and Leas of the Alban Institute write, "that most of the churches which were successfully finding and integrating new members had some kind of outreach into the community."[19]

Institute the Process for the Formation of New Christians

The fifth characteristic of an evangelizing church is that it has established a process for the formation of new Christians. A compelling conclusion on church growth by the Alban Institute is that "a newcomer is much more likely to 'stick' if he or she has a place to go, a place where he or she is known and would be missed if she or he does not attend." "Friendship ties," the research shows, is the "strongest bonding agent for helping members stick to a congregation."[20]

One of the remarkable features of *Journey to Jesus* is that it is a context for lifelong friendships. Conversion occurs in a social context. The purpose of the sevenfold process of conversion and integration into Christ and the church is to bring a person into a conscious, active, and intentional relationship with Christ through the community of his body, the church. Conversion is not individualistic, it is communal. Consequently, friendship and relationship is not a by-product of the conversion process, but is integral to it. The new Christian is not asked to "attend" church but to enter into the congregation and live out of the church as the central community of his or her life. We enter into the life of God through the life of God's earthly community, living under the reign of Christ.

What kind of outreach group should you begin? I have no statistics on this matter, but my hunch is that the primary crisis faced in our Western postmodern world is the loss of meaning and values. Therefore, "outreach groups" that target sources of the loss of meaning and values will "connect" with people who are ripe for conversion. Ask the people of the church. They will identify the specific needs of the congregation and of the area in which you minister. Establish groups that meet these specific, local needs.

To summarize, there are five characteristics of the church that will attract and evangelize the seeker:

(1) a church that understands its missional nature
(2) a church that is a renewed, vital, and energetic embodiment of faith
(3) a church where every member is committed to inviting people in their own social network to "come and see"
(4) a church that has gained a reputation for "reaching out" to help people in need;
(5) a church that adapts the fourfold process of *conversion, discipleship, equipping,* and *incorporation* into the church. The process takes the seeker by the hand and

leads him or her into a deep and lifelong commitment to Christ and the church.

A striking, and I think, attractive feature about ancient evangelism adapted to the postmodern world is that it is not an easy-believism. It stands against the cultural tendency to pass in and out of various belief systems. It says in a loving, gracious and embracing way "take up their cross and follow me" (Matt. 16:24), for "I am the way, and the truth, and the life" (John 14:6). This is the message of Christianity and it cannot be weakened to "I am one of many ways." In *The Finality of Christ,* Lesslie Newbigin has shown that "to claim finality for Jesus Christ is not to assert either that the majority of men will some day be Christians, or to assert that all others will be damned. It is to claim that commitment to him is the way in which men can become truly aligned to the ultimate end for which all things were made. The Church which believes this will not be afraid to address confidently to every generation . . . the call which it has received from him: Follow me."[21]

Once the seeker has made a commitment to "follow me," the seeker comes into a new relationship with the church through the rite of welcome, a rite that expresses their initial conversion to Christ.

6. The Rite of Conversion

One of my most vivid childhood memories is of my longing to become a Boy Scout. The local Boy Scout group met next door in the church where my father pastored. Every Friday evening for years I watched the bigger boys come to the Scout meeting decorated in their official uniforms. I hung around the church, peeking in the windows at the games, the serious discussion, and the fun this society of fortunate people enjoyed. When they left on their scouting trips, I was there to help them pack and to wave good-bye. And when they returned, I was there to welcome them, help them unpack, and listen to their camping stories with wonderment and jealousy. I kept track of the months, the weeks, and even the days as I approached the magic age of twelve. Finally, the day came when I could join the Scouts. The meeting for the induction of the new Boy Scouts was held in the woods behind the church, in an open patch of grass by a small stream. It was a warm summer evening, a gentle breeze was blowing, and the sky was filled with stars. We sat around a sparkling fire, singing songs and listening to stories about selfless Boy Scouts becoming men of honor and influence. Then, in a solemn ceremony of induction, our names were called out and we stepped forward to hear the words of welcome and admonition, to receive the Boy Scout handshake, and then to join the others in the Scout's oath. My dream had come true. I could now begin a new journey, a journey within a journey, one of learning and fun, and of challenges and accomplishments in the Boy Scout community. The passage rite was the gate leading into the next stage of the journey.

Every journey is characterized by turning points. As we acknowledge the significance of these turning points, we create rites to symbolize and commemorate them. A passage rite symbolizes a transition from one period of development to another. Consider the rites that have developed around birthdays, graduations, engagements, weddings, and anniversaries. These rites shape and enhance our personal histories. Without them, life would be less exciting and less secure. Similarly, our development in faith may be characterized by rites of religious passage that embody and communicate the event they symbolize.

The Evangelical community has always recognized the value of conversion rites. I grew up in a church where we had the yearly ritual of an evangelism week. I've also been to the Billy Graham Crusades and many other similar evangelistic causes. All of these events end with a ritual: "If you want to accept Jesus as your Savior, raise your hand. . . . Now, while Christians are praying, walk down front and speak to a counselor." A ritual is performative. It is remembered as an "event," a "turning point" in life.

Ritual theory recognizes that performative symbols especially relate to rites of separation, rites of transition, and rites of incorporation.[1] The passage rite of conversion separates a person from his or her former way of life. It's a rite of transition to a new way of life and incorporation into a new community.

The Rite of Welcome in the Ancient Church

The passage rite of welcome is important because of what it *says and demands.* In words and gestures it says the gospel. It orders and organizes a spiritual experience around the gospel. But it also demands faith, intention, and response. Like a coin, worship is composed of two sides. On one side, God speaks and acts. But on the other, we must respond to God and to each other. This form evokes, elicits, and defines the inner response of the human heart.

Like all rites, the rite of welcome was a passage from one state or condition to another. In the ancient church, this rite took a converting person from the seeker path of evangelism to the hearer path of discipleship. It dealt with the heart and expressed the transfer of allegiance from the kingdom of this world to the reign of God in the church. Without an inner response, the form is ritualism; but with an inner response, it is rite in the biblical and best meaning of the term.

No detailed description of the rite of welcome has been recorded by the church fathers. However, sufficient evidence demonstrates that the rite was in existence in the third century. In *The Apostolic Tradition*, Hippolytus depicts a rite of welcome: "New converts to the faith, who are to be admitted to hearers of the word, shall first be brought to the teachers before the people assemble. And they shall be examined as to their reason for embracing the faith, and they who bring them shall testify that they are competent to hear the word."[2] Several decades after Hippolytus wrote these words, Origen, the head of a Christian school in Alexandria gave more evidence of the rite. In his writing to Celsus, a pagan philosopher who had attacked Christianity, Origen defended the Christian approach to maturation against that of the philosophers. He claimed that the philosophers talked to anyone who would listen and thus had no organized way of leading their hearers into truth. By comparison, the Christians had a series of graduated steps that led a person into instruction, connected by a passage rite of conversion for those who were "receiving admission."[3] This passage rite consisted of four parts. The seeker is signed, hands are placed upon the head, salt is given to the seeker, and the pastor breathes upon him or her.

The first of these parts was the *signing*. The signing—in which each candidate received the sign of the cross on the forehead—signified that the candidate belonged to Christ, whose sign (the cross) he or she bore. The second part of the rite, the *laying on of hands*, usually accompanied the signing. It pointed to a relationship of dependence upon the church: the one who comes to Christ must come to Christ through the church. The third part is the *presentation of salt* to the candidates. While a variety of meanings may have been assigned to this rite, it essentially served as a sign of hospitality, a welcome into the community of faith. It may also have symbolized the calling to be the salt of the earth, or reminded the convert of purification and wisdom. Finally, the fourth part is the *rite of breathing*. Although references to this rite are scarce, the meaning may be related to blowing away evil spirits and receiving the Holy Spirit.[4]

What is of primary importance here is that these rites supported the main emphasis of the rite of conversion, which signified separation from evil, from paganism, and from the old life while transitioning into a new life in Christ and the church. Consequently, the rite of welcome is seen as a type of exodus or even as conception in the womb of the church.[5]

The Passage Rite of Conversion Today

Even today, the passage rite from seeker to hearer is a very important milestone in the spiritual journey of the converting person. The congregation needs to value this moment not only for the seeker but also for itself. The rite points to the crucial part members of a congregation play as communal mentors, and speaks to the commitment each is to hold and express in the way he or she lives. For this reason I suggest that the ancient rite of welcome be seen as a *rite of conversion*.

The rite of conversion occurs in a regular service of worship. The seekers assemble at the back of the sanctuary with their mentors. The mentors stand behind the seekers and place hands on the seekers' back or shoulders. Then the pastor asks each seeker to give his or her name and to state why he or she is there and what is desired. The pastor then proclaims the gospel and the promise of new life to those who receive Jesus Christ as personal Lord and Savior.

Next, the seekers renounce all association with pagan ideologies and habits and commit solely to the worship of the tri-une God. This may be expressed by the symbol of breathing upon the candidate. Then the seekers step forward to receive the sign of the cross on the forehead, ears, eyes, lips, breast-bone, and shoulder. This action symbolizes that the whole person belongs to Christ. Finally, the seekers are invited to enter into the church and to be seated among the faithful. They sit among the faithful with their mentors at their side.

These various steps verbalize and dramatize the action of moving from the condition of unbelief to belief. Both the action of God and the response of the people are important. The action of God is verbally expressed in the first promise. Here the leader reviews what God has done to provide salvation. This is followed by the renunciation of non-Christian worship, which dramatically proclaims the candidates' allegiance to Jesus Christ. This is a performative symbol. As Regis Duffy has stated, "The church has never simply taught the paschal mystery. Rather she has always invited and enabled Christians to participate in that mystery."[6] This truth is expressed in the ancient saying, "*lex orandi, lex credendi*" (the law of worship is the law of belief). The rite of conversion points to the most fundamental issue of evangelism—repenting, and entering into a new life in Christ and the community of the church. It explains life at its deepest level and brings a person into the experience of community. As the whole congregation participates in the rite of conversion, a recurring ceremony of conversion and nurturing into the Christian faith results. This resembles the annual revival meetings held in rural churches. Not only are new converts brought into the church, but established members are also called into a renewed dedication to the faith and to the church.

The conversion rite is not a mere ritualistic form. It expresses the converting person's transfer into faith, confirms the covenant God is making with him or her, and elicits a response. It is not a gimmick or a device, but an embodiment of the relationship being established between God and the seeker. It presents Christ as victor over sin and death, communicates the mysteries of salvation, and represents a step into a new period of conversion—instruction in the faith in which the seeker becomes a disciple.

Suggestions on How to Conduct
the Rite of Conversion
USE THESE RITES AS PRESENTED OR DEVELOP YOUR OWN.

1. The pastor stands at the back of the church and summons the seekers and their mentors to stand with the pastor.
2. The pastor proclaims the nature of repentance and faith as a turning away from all evil.
3. The pastor then leads the seekers in the words of renunciation and turning to Jesus. [The words below are intended to serve as guidelines. They may be addressed to each individual by name if the group is small, or to the whole group if it is large.]

Question: Do you confess you are a sinner in need of reconciliation with God?

Answer: I do.

Question: Do you believe in Jesus Christ for the forgiveness of your sin?

Answer: I do.

Question: Do you renounce Satan and all the spiritual forces of wickedness that rebel against God?

Answer: I renounce them.

Question: Do you renounce the evil powers of this world which corrupt and destroy the creatures of God?

Answer: I renounce them.

Question: Do you renounce all sinful desires that draw you from the love of God?

Answer: I renounce them.

Question: Do you turn to Jesus Christ and accept him as your Savior?

Answer: I do.

Question: Do you put your whole trust in his grace and love?

Answer: I do.

Question: Do you promise to follow and obey him as your Lord?

Answer: I do.

(*Book of Common Prayer*, pp. 302-3
except for first two questions)

Silence is kept for a short period of time as the pastor prepares the rituals that symbolize conversion and welcome into the church.

4. The pastor now does the following performative symbols (or others), preferably with each person. If the group is large, gestures may be directed toward the congregation.

- The pastor traces the *sign of the cross* on the seeker's forehead (or hands the seeker a cross) and says, "Take up your cross and follow Jesus."
- The pastor *lays hands on the head* of the seeker and says, "You belong to the church. . . . You are now part of this spiritual community."
- The pastor *hands the seeker a Bible*, saying, "This book is the source of wisdom. Read it. Mark it. Learn it. Live by it."
- The pastor then *breathes into the face* of the seeker and says, "You have been given the Holy Spirit. Live by the fruits of the Spirit—love, joy, peace, patience, kindness, goodness, faithfulness, gentleness, and self-control."

5. The pastor may say words of welcome to the entire group, or to each individual if the group is small enough. The congregation may respond by clapping or some other sign of approval and welcome.

6. The final performative symbol of conversion is for the seeker and mentor to walk from the back of the church into the congregation and take a seat among the faithful.

In this section I have introduced historic evangelism and shown how the principles may be adapted into our current context. This evangelism touches the whole person and calls for new allegiances of the heart and mind. It begins with personal contact, and brings a person into a community of loving and committed people who model the spirit of true Christianity for the newcomer. The rite of conversion is a powerful symbol of renouncing all that is sin and death and of turning to Jesus and the church where the new Christian is warmly received and will be nurtured by the community into a lifelong commitment to Christ. The seeker has now become a disciple and will be nurtured from within the community by worship and Scripture study into a deeper faith. And he or she will experience the formation of Christian character through personal and small group discipleship.

Leader's Guide

A. EVALUATE
- Could we present the gospel more clearly?
- Do we have a missional self-understanding?
- How could we become a more healthy, vibrant, birthing, and nurturing community?
- How can we encourage our congregation to become more effective in witnessing in their social networks?
- What do we need to do to enhance our "reputation" in this community?
- Should a core group go through the *Journey to Jesus* before reaching out to others?

B. PLANNING A COURSE OF ACTION TO REVITALIZE THE CONGREGATION
Create a "focus group" consisting of a cross section of your church (age, sex, culture) and ask them the above questions. Listen carefully to their answers.

C. PLANNING A COURSE OF ACTION FOR EVANGELIZING THE SEEKER

- Encourage an every-member evangelism.
- Develop a class to teach people how to share faith.
- Examine *Follow Me!* (Wheaton, Ill.: IWS Resources, 2001) to determine its effectiveness for your approach.

Resources for Further Reading

A suggested resource for the seeker is *Follow Me!* (Wheaton, Ill.: IWS Resources, 2001). Suggested resources for the leaders include Rodney Stark, *The Rise of Christianity* (San Francisco: HarperCollins, 1997), a sociological study of how Christianity defeated paganism; Kevin Graham Ford, *Jesus for a New Generation* (Downers Grove: InterVarsity Press, 1995), which is especially helpful in understanding ministry to Generation X and Millennials; Eddie Gibbs, *ChurchNext: Quantum Changes in How We Do Ministry* (Downers Grove: InterVarsity Press, 2000), thoughtful good insight on the church in a postmodern world; Francis Kelly Nemeck and Marie Theresa Coombs, *The Way of Spiritual Direction* (Collegeville, Minn.: Liturgical Press, 1985), a must-read for all who will mentor; Christine Pohl, *Making Room: Recovering Hospitality as a Christian Tradition* (Grand Rapids: Eerdmans, 1994), a crucial read for churches that want to embody the spirit of evangelism; and Lee Strobel, *The Case for Christ: A Journalist's Personal Investigation of the Evidence for Jesus* (Grand Rapids: Zondervan, 1998).

III

Discipling
the Hearer

TEACHING THE NEW BELIEVER

JOURNEY TO JESUS

HEARER

Spiritual Goal:
  Discipleship
Passage Rite:
  Rite of
  Covenant
Resource:
  Be My Disciple!

INTRODUCTION

I first met Steve in 1968—my first year teaching at Wheaton College—during the third session of my course on Christian thought. Steve distinguished himself in that class by publicly announcing that he did not believe in God. "We work on two different presuppositions," he declared. "You believe in God; I do not." Immediately after class I caught his eye and shouted, "Steve, wait for me. I want to talk with you!"

I found out that Steve was Jewish and had been brought up on the streets of Brooklyn. At an early age he was streetwise and tough. Like Saul of Tarsus, his life was turned around because someone dared to witness to him. Unlike Saul, Steve was turned into an instant celebrity. "Look at what the gospel can do," they said. "It can take a kid right off the streets and instantly transform him." Steve was a trophy, an evangelical success story, a miracle. In no time at all he was the featured speaker in youth gatherings and in Sunday night services in the New York area. People were so impressed with him that they raised enough money to send him to a Christian college.

But several years later, Steve was not only an unbeliever but a cynic. What happened to this trophy? Why the change? In one of many intimate conversations, Steve confessed that he had never been baptized. "Why?" I asked. "The commitment was more than I could handle," he admitted. "Were you ever instructed in the faith?" I asked. "Not really," he answered. I have often wondered whether it was the lack of discipleship that caused Steve to lose faith. Was Steve unable to grow in the faith because he had not experienced a period of nurturing?

The second stage in the Journey to Jesus is a time of formation and instruction and is the womb-like period for the newly

93

conceived Christian. It is a time to be nurtured, cared for, and formed by the Word. It is a time of spiritual growth. But unlike the seeker period, when the growth takes place primarily outside the Christian community, the growth now occurs inside the womb of the church. By "outside the church" I do not mean that the seeker was not in church during the seeker period; I refer instead to the absence of commitment. The rite of conversion is a ritual of commitment that moves a seeker from an observant, looking in from the outside, to the inside where seeking is replaced with committed hearing under the tutelage of a spiritual mentor or small group. The rite of conversion is a public expression of faith. To use the new-life image, it is the conception. Now the converting person is in the womb of the church where growth, like that of gestation, occurs.

The theme of discipleship finds its origin in Jesus and his twelve disciples and then again in the example of Paul and Timothy. Paul instructs Timothy to pass on what had been handed down to him: "And the things you have heard me say in the presence of many witnesses entrust to reliable men who will also be qualified to teach others" (2 Tim. 2:2 NIV).

Walter Henrichsen reminds us that "disciples are made, not born." The spiritual mentor is advised: "When we invest in the lives of other people, we transmit not only what we know but, more importantly, what we are. . . . Teaching others . . . entails the imparting of a life—the same in-depth transmission that occurred between Paul and Timothy."[1]

7. Discipleship in the Ancient Church

Discipling New Christians in the New Testament

In some churches, baptisms are conducted after every service of worship for the people who responded that day to the preaching of Christ. The argument for immediate baptism is drawn from Acts, from the accounts in which conversion and baptism apparently occur without any intervening time. Most examples of baptism in the New Testament do imply immediate baptism. But some passages of Scripture suggest that converts were put through a period of training before they were baptized. It may be that those converted from the Hebrew background were baptized immediately, while those from pagan backgrounds needed a longer period of time for spiritual growth and development before baptism.

An example of an immediate baptism is found in the conversion of the Ethiopian eunuch (Acts 8:26-40). A longer period of preparation more than likely preceded the baptism. The eunuch was already deeply rooted in the religion of Israel; he was reading the book of Isaiah, and sensed that he did not yet understand what his heart grasped. Consequently, God directed Philip to go to him and to witness in such a way that the journey into faith the eunuch had been making for sometime would take a dramatic turn. Because of his journey and readiness for conversion, he was baptized then and there by Philip.

Support for an evangelism that consisted of various stages of commitment and knowledge is suggested in the book of Hebrews. A journey that goes beyond the preliminary hearing of the gospel is implied in the distinction made between milk and solid food in Hebrews 6. This sense of a journey is buttressed by the admonition to "leave the elementary doctrines of Christ and go on to maturity" (Heb. 6:1 RSV). Certainly, this text implies stages, steps, growth, process, and development. Christians, like newborn babes, are not to remain in arrested development. No, like a parent, the writer of Hebrews was calling newborn babes into a journey toward maturity, beyond an arrested faith.

There are additional materials in the New Testament that imply a period of time for learning and adapting to the new way of life demanded by baptism (see Col. 3:8–4:12; Eph. 4:22–6:19; 1 Pet. 1:1–4:11; 1 Pet. 4:12–5:14; James 1:1–4:10). What were new believers taught? Philip Carrington, in *The Primitive Christian Catechism*, points to four teachings included in the catechetical materials of the New Testament:

(1) *deponenter* (new Christians were taught to put off evil)
(2) *subjecti* (new Christians were taught to submit to God and each other)
(3) *vigilate* (new Christians were taught to watch and pray)
(4) *resistite* (new Christians were taught to resist the devil)

These themes are seen in Ephesians:
(1) "Put on the new nature, created after the likeness of God in true righteousness and holiness. . . . Therefore, putting away falsehood" (Eph. 4:24-25 RSV).
(2) "Be subject to one another" (Eph. 5:21).
(3) "Put on the whole armor of God" (Eph. 6:11*a*).
(4) "That you may be able to stand against the wiles of the devil" (Eph. 6:11*b*).[1]

These prebaptismal teachings touch on attitudes and values that go to the very heart of Christian spirituality. They describe the journey from paganism to Christian faith, a movement away from a former way of life, from former commitments and values, to a new life and new values. The convert journeys into a new community of people, a people who live in submission to God and to each other, battle the forces of evil, and stand against the devil in the name of Jesus, the victor over the devil's domain and power.

It takes time for pagans to enter into this community—time for formation, time for the acquisition of new values, time for the transfer of allegiance from worldly powers to the power of Christ working through his body, the church. In the third century, these persons were called hearers.

Discipling in the Ancient Church

The third-century writer Hippolytus tells a great deal about discipling in the early church. The period of instruction could extend as long as three years. If a person's faith and conduct showed more rapid formation, he or she proceeded more quickly into the full life of the church.[2]

In the third century, the first phase of discipleship took place in the worship service itself. The *hearers* were in worship for the reading of Scripture and the sermon. In A.D. 150, Justin Martyr described the service of the word as when "the memoirs of the apostles or the writings of the prophets are read, as long as time permits . . . , when the reader has finished, the president in a discourse urges and invites us to the imitation of these noble things."[3] After the sermon, the *hearers* were dismissed to another room where they reflected on the Scripture reading and sermon. During this time, the faithful (a term used of the committed and baptized members of the community) remained in the worship space where they prayed and celebrated the Eucharist.

What was going on for the *hearers* while the rest of the

congregation continued worship? It was a time to learn the essentials of the faith reflected in the assembly of the community, in the worship of the church, and in the reading and preaching of Scripture. But what did all this mean?

The third-century fathers of the church assigned images to capture the essence of this particular phase of Christian discipleship. One very prominent image is that of the soldier. Third-century fathers such as Tertullian, Cyprian, and Commodian frequently described discipleship as analogous to the training soldiers underwent. To become a soldier, a person had to go through stages of development. The recruit began as a *tiro*, a novice who had to spend time in an apprenticeship learning how to use his weapons and equipment before becoming a soldier. Once his proficiency had been proved, an oath to serve, even at the cost of his life, was taken. This oath was sealed by the tattoo of his superior.

Like the Roman soldier, the disciple was to renounce his or her pagan background and enter an apprenticeship in which training in the weapons of God against Satan was given. This image of military training points to the *Christus Victor* theme that dominates the worldview of the third century. Christ, the victor over sin, death, and the dominion of Satan, was calling recruits into his community, the church, the sign of his victory in the world. Their calling was to live the life of victory over sin in the context of a pagan world. And through this new life, witness was made against the powers of evil.

A second highly popular image of the *hearer* is the Old Testament exodus. Origen of Alexandria compared Israel's departure from Egypt for the promised land to the rejection of paganism and acceptance of Christ. The crossing of the Red Sea was analogous to the seekers' rite of welcome into the church. The *hearer* is then likened to the sojourn of Israel in the wilderness. Here, the one being discipled heard the law of God, and, as with Moses, the glory of God was revealed. This image of the Exodus was meant to encourage the pilgrim to endure to the end. It is not merely incidental that the journey of Israel was a journey of people together. For the journey into Christ, like Israel, is the journey of a people who support, assist, and encourage each other on the way.

The third and the most popular image of the *hearer* is that of gestation and birth. The candidate is conceived in the womb of the church by the Word of God. Discipleship is the period of gestation, the time of formation and development in the womb. In this environment, the infant is given tender, loving care, nursed, coddled, and nourished into maturity. This image emphasizes formation, development, process, and growth. Furthermore, it stresses new life in the context of family and community. The early church knew no such thing as an individualistic Christianity—it practiced evangelism by, in, and through the community of God's people.

8. Discipleship Today

Turning from the world of the early church, we now ask how the ancient approach to the *hearer* may be adopted and put to use in discipleship today. The hearer stage is an integral part of the spiritual process because it solidifies what began in the seeker stage. Like the child being formed in the womb, the new convert experiences a period of gestation and prenatal development to have a spiritual birth. In order for this stage to be effective, three conditions must occur:

- the *right image of discipleship*
- a *womb-like atmosphere*
- a *content that fits* this early stage of development

The Right Image of Discipleship

The right image of discipleship is Jesus. The convert is called to be like him and no other.

Since 1970 there has been a renewed interest in finding a hero to emulate. Curiously, this new interest represents a contradiction. On the one hand, society holds up individualism as a virtue to be pursued with vengeance. On the other hand, there is a longing among people to "get connected" with a hero, especially in a spiritual way. James Fowler refers to this second drive as a call to "a spirituality of vocation."[1]

Fowler understands the "spirituality of vocation" in relation to several shifts taking place in society, particularly in regard to what constitutes the image of a good man or good woman. According to Fowler, prior to 1950 our hero image focused on the ethic of self-denial, but since the

1960s the focus is on the ethic of self-fulfillment.[2] A good example of this shift is found in the Evangelical world. The heroes of the 1950s were a group of missionaries killed while attempting to reach the Auca Indians in South America. These young men—five of them and especially Jim Elliot, who had written about a self-giving life while in college—were extolled as great examples to follow. At Wheaton College, where two of the five (Jim Elliot and Ed McCully) graduated and Nate Saint attended, bronze statues were placed in the chapel, dormitories were named after them, and books were written extolling their virtues. But in the latter part of the twentieth century these great heroes of the faith are nearly forgotten, while the new heroes are the pastors of the megachurches and leaders of movements within the church who have actualized their potential and become self-fulfilled gurus of the Evangelical enterprises.

The image of the hero has undergone great change in not only the church but also in society. For example, when I was a boy, a hero was someone who had given himself or herself for a great cause. I grew up after World War II with the image of the military hero in particular. Men like President Eisenhower and Winston Churchill were not "just war heroes," they were the great men of the world because they had sacrificed their personal lives for duty to their country and service to the peoples of the world. Today's heroes are those who have achieved success in the entertainment or athletic world. They are the self-achievers. They have worked hard and paid a personal price for their own success. Consequently, they have become our cultural icons, our images to follow, our examples of a fulfilled life. Interestingly, in the midst of all the popularity surrounding personal achievement, the longing to discover the inner and spiritual side of the self has emerged. In order to understand this contradiction, Fowler points to the work of psycho-historian Robert Jay Lifton, who has studied "the relationship between large-scale historical change and individual patterns of adaptation."[3] Lifton has found that the dislocation we all feel because of the momentous changes in culture have resulted in this inner longing for the recovery of authentic meaning. These two realities "pull powerfully at each other in the hearts of each of us and in the culture of which we are a part."[4] We are enamored with superficial cultural icons, yet drawn to an authentic inner self.

The new convert who enters into the discipleship stage of the evangelism process feels this same tension. On the one hand, the disciple may have entertainment or athletic heroes, but, on the other hand, he or she experiences an inner need and drive for a spiritual hero, a person to emulate who fulfills a spiritual need. Therefore the resurgence of the discipleship movement needs to be understood within the realities of our present moment in history. The icons of culture and the nostalgia for the past are pulling all of us in two directions. The images of culture and the longing of the heart are in conflict.

For this reason it is of utmost importance for spiritual mentors to direct hearers to biblical heroes of the faith while encouraging them in their commitment to serve. The goal of discipleship is not to become a "hero" in the church for one's own power or recognition. The true image of discipleship is servanthood, a giving of self with no expectation of return. When Jesus discipled his followers, he taught that "everyone who exalts himself will be humbled, and he who humbles himself will be exalted" (Luke 14:11 NIV). The disciple is called to be like Jesus, who came not to be served but to serve. The right image is "the servanthood of Jesus." The disciple is called to follow Jesus in servanthood leadership (see Phil. 2:6-11).

Discipleship is not a vocation prescribed only for ministers and other full-time staff members in the church. Discipleship is the full-time spiritual vocation of *all* God's people. Time in discipleship is time to impress upon the new convert that he or she has a calling in Jesus Christ—the calling to be a disciple all the time and in every place of life.

The Womb-like Atmosphere of Discipleship

If the new convert is to grow, he or she needs a womb-like experience for a period of initial gestation. This can occur in a personal "one-on-one" relationship or in a small group. First, in a *one-on-one* relationship, the person doing the discipleship is called a *spiritual mentor*. This may be the same person who initiated a relationship with the seeker and was instrumental in bringing the seeker into the church, or it may be another person assigned to the seeker. The work of the spiritual mentor is not that of a "mentoring committee," but a calling. Not everybody has this particular calling. I don't. Students have asked me to mentor them and I reply, "It's not my calling, I'll be glad to meet with you once in a while to chat about things, but what you really need is someone who is called to be a spiritual director, someone who has trained for that specific ministry." In each congregation where the Worship, Evangelism, and Nurture Mission has been initiated, there will be those called to the ministry of spiritual mentor. Because the work of the spiritual mentor is so crucial in discipleship, it is important that only those who are called and trained in this ministry should be assigned to the hearer.[5]

The second fruitful context for the discipleship is the *small group*. The small group phenomena has recently spread throughout the world like wildfire and is found everywhere in society from various self-help programs to the church. Robert Wuthnow, in *"I Come Away Stronger,"* writes: "In recent years, religious leaders have been paying increasing attention to small groups. Bible studies, prayer fellowships, house churches, and covenant groups are being touted as the wave of the future. They are the settings in which lonely people, yearning for community, can find support and encouragement. Their members can care for each other, pray with one another, work together on community projects, and spark vitality in religious institutions."[6] Wuthnow's research included a follow-up book, *Sharing the Journey*. His work has become the foundation for understanding how the small group encourages spiritual growth and provides insights on the *process* by which this spiritual formation occurs.

The small group leader, like the spiritual mentor, needs to approach group leading from the sense of calling. Leading a small group of *hearers* and discipling them in the faith is a highly important ministry. As Wuthnow points out, the twentieth century has been characterized by shallow or superficial religious commitments, thus creating a society increasingly subject to secularity. In this circumstance, small groups are likely to be regarded as a new force, stemming the tide of disbelief and moral relativism.[7]

THE CONTENT OF THE HEARER PHASE

What should the hearer be taught in this "womb-like" time? Three things:

- What does it mean to be the church?
- What do we do in worship?
- How should I read Scripture?

Parker Palmer, one of America's most noted Christian educators, argues that authentic education can be summarized in the following statement: "To teach is to create a space in which the community of truth is practiced."[8] He goes on to declare that "we now see that to know something is to have a living relationship with it."[9] The goal of all Christian discipleship is not just the imparting of knowledge, but also a relationship with God, the source of all knowledge. For this reason, a disciple's formation must not start with objective knowledge about the faith, but with a reflection on the experience of faith. Discipleship begins as the hearer experiences and reflects on the community of truth (the Church), the proclamation and celebration of truth (worship) and the source of truth (the Scripture). The goal, as Palmer suggests, is to guide the hearer into "a living relationship." The booklets prepared by the Institute for Worship Studies follow the Parker principle. The specific booklet for this stage of growth is entitled *Be My Disciple!*[10] It guides the convert into a deeper relationship with God through a discussion and reflection on what it means to be the church, to worship, and to read Scripture.

What Does It Mean to Be the Church?

The first task of the spiritual mentor is to help the hearer develop a living relationship with the church. What does it mean to be in the church? How does being in the church disciple and form a person as a new hearer? These answers should come from a combination of biblical teaching and the experience of being a part of the Christian community.

Biblical teaching about the church is important. Here the new convert is exposed to the teaching of the Bible on what it means to be the church. This kind of teaching occurs in small Bible study groups and deals with the church as a theological idea. The church is God's people, the fellowship of faith, the new creation, the body of Christ. All these images can be explored for their meaning. Discussions may be enlightening, stretching, and encouraging. Probing these images is a vital part of learning to be church; but to be fully aware of what it means to be church, the community must put theory into practice. This practical kind of knowledge will be communication through study of what the Scripture teaches about the church.

The second kind of "knowing what it means to be

church" is much more indirect and is related to the kind of communications that occurs in tribes through their shared symbols and stories told and embodied within their communities. The latter has been rediscovered in the postmodern world and is reshaping our view of how the church forms disciples.[11]

The church, like a tribe, is a cultural community defined by the story of God. This story and shared vision is taught and communicated primarily as a lived experience. When a convert enters into the Christian community and becomes a disciple of Jesus, the person confesses that life is defined by the story of Israel and Jesus. Therefore it is important during the disciple stage to experience the biblical nature of the church. The church is not a mere voluntary society of like-minded believers, but a continuation of the presence of Jesus in and to the world. It is the "body of Christ," the real extension and continuation of the incarnation, death, resurrection, and anticipated return of Christ. Therefore the church belongs to the narrative of God's activity in the world. To come into the church is to come into the locus of God's presence. The church not only has a story of God's saving presence and grace, it *is* the present actualization of the story. To participate in the church is to be discipled by its self-understanding, ethic, and vision. Therefore the very essence of the Christian faith is not only taught but caught by the *hearer*.[12]

The disciple is asked to "catch" the biblical understanding of the church as it is presented by Paul in Ephesians. The theological nature of the church as a continuation of the presence of Jesus in the world and as a witness to the "rulers and authorities" call the people of God into a special relationship with God and each other. The reading and reflection on Ephesians will make faith real as the *hearer* experiences the reality of the church through the sense of belonging, openness, caring, cooperation, healing, forgiveness, patience, trust, the freedom to be oneself, weakness, the use of gifts, and the conviction that the community does not exist for the individual, but the individual exists for the community.[13] These are the shared values of a local church committed not only to talking about community, but being community. The church is a new culture. It is not to be like the world, where principalities and powers strive to make communities exclusive, closed, uncaring, uncooperative, destructive, unforgiving, impatient, and incapable of trust, and force people into a one-size-fits-all mold and to become power hungry. Rodney Clapp reminds us: "The original Christians, in short, were about creating and sustaining a unique culture—a way of life that would shape character in the image of their God. And they were determined to be a culture, . . . even if it killed them and their children."[14]

The congregation that pays attention to its inner life will make an impact in its outer communication. It will become, to use the phrase of Willard Swartley and Donald Kraybill, the "community of compassion." This understanding of the church and its outward ministry to believers and to the world is captured in the words of Menno Simons, the sixteenth-century Anabaptist leader whose name marks the Mennonite community:

> We do not teach and practice community of goods. But we teach and maintain by the word of the Lord that all truly believing Christians are members of one body and are baptized by one spirit into one body (1 Cor. 12:13); they are partakers of one bread (1 Cor. 10:18), they have one Lord and one God (Eph. 4:5-6). . . . All those . . . called into one body and love in Christ Jesus, are prepared by such love to serve their neighbors, not only with money and goods, but also after the example of their Lord and head, Jesus Christ, in an evangelical manner with life and blood.[15]

This kind of church—an embodied continuation of the presence of Jesus in the world—is a healthy, vibrant community of people. By its very existence it is able to transmit to the hearer a vital, committed, transmission of what it means to be a participant in the community of Jesus.

What Does It Mean to Worship?

Second, during this period of growth, the *hearer* is taught *the meaning of worship*. As new Christians are discipled in worship, attention must be paid to the proper place of the individual in worship. For decades, the instrumental approach toward worship dominated modernity. This approach focused too much on what effect worship has on the worshiper, a "me"-centered worship.

Recent worship studies have taken the focus off the individual and placed it back on the triune God.[16] Triune worship places worship in the proper perspective. Worship is not directed toward human need. Instead, it is, as in the words of the earliest eucharistic liturgy, a ministry to God. Hippolytus, in *The Apostolic Tradition* (c. A.D. 215), writes: "Giving you thanks because you have held us worthy to stand before you and minister to you."[17] The disciple needs to be taught that in the ministry of praise, we enter into a relationship with the Father through the language of mystery, with the Son through the language of story, and with the Holy Spirit through the language of symbol.

True worship is not about me. It is not about my knowledge, my experience, my healing, my empowerment. True worship proclaims and enacts the narrative of God's story. It is about the God of character, the God who is just, righteous, holy, merciful, and loving. It is about the God who acts, the God who creates a good world, the God who mourns over a world gone astray, the God who rescues the world—not by power but by weakness. It is about the God who cannot be contained in all the heavens, yet became contained in the womb of the Virgin Mary, born of her the Savior of the world. Worship is about the God who does for us what we cannot do for ourselves. It thankfully remembers how God became incarnate as the second Adam to reverse the human situation. He who knew no sin became one of us, and took on the consequence of our sin, death. By death he destroyed death, restored the nature of humanity and opened the way to heaven.

As the Scriptures declare and as the liturgies of the early church attest, authentic worship first and foremost signifies God's saving mission to the world. This is the mission of the triune God. Worship is *leiturgia* (the work of the church), in which the church proclaims and enacts God's saving mission to the world. It sings it, praises it, reads it, preaches it, thankfully remembers it at the table and goes forth to live in its awareness and reality. This is the purpose of worship, the goal of worship and the end of worship. It has to do with God—God's creation, work in history, and goal for humanity and the whole cosmic order. We did not invent, create, or establish God's saving act for the world. Our calling as God's people on earth is to bear witness to God's mission to the world, to be thankful for it, to be shaped by it, and to live it. When these truths are proclaimed and enacted, worship disciples the convert into Christian truth. It forms the *hearer's* perspective on life and shapes a view of reality. The disciple needs to know that he or she has been created for worship and finds fulfillment in being a person at worship.

But there is also a subjective side to worship, a disposition the *hearer* brings to worship—a converted heart. The heart continually says, "Just as I am without one plea, but that thy blood was shed for me." This heart is willing to "take up your cross and follow [Jesus]." It is an open, teachable, vulnerable, and thankful heart, one that loves to hear the old, old story. This heart assembles in worship with intention. The body worships, the mind worships; the whole person is at heartfelt worship. This intentional worship inevitably leads to participatory worship. Worship is not done to us or for us. It is not a concert, a lecture, or a rally. Worship is a verb.[18] It is done by us—it is, as the documents of Vatican II describe, "full, conscious, and active participation." This is dialogic worship. The hearer stands in respect, sits to listen, kneels in humility, sings from the heart, engages in gesture, responds, and receives the laying on of hands, the anointing of oil, and the prayer for healing. In all of these actions, worship creates the experience of awe and wonder, the sense of the ineffable, reverence, godly fear, awareness of the total otherness of the God who cannot be known, yet the sense of the presence of the mystery of the One who is closer than a brother or sister.

In sum, the *hearer* needs to learn authentic worship. First, God acts: what God has done in history to rescue the world, the *Missio Dei,* is signified and re-presented. Second, God's people respond. They participate in the unfolding drama. The result is that the God of creation, incarnation, and re-creation is glorified, and the community of God on earth is shaped into the presence of Christ in a particular time, place, and history. In this kind of worship, the *hearer* is formed and shaped toward a live and active Christian commitment.

Worship maintains and deepens the relationship already established with God. The new convert develops a relationship to transcendence, to the spiritual side of reality, to the mystery that is fundamental to the universe. This cannot be taught only in an intellectual way. Relationship with God through prayer, spiritual hearing of the Word, and interaction with the worshiping community cannot be exhausted in a classroom lecture or on a blackboard diagram. It has to happen. It has to be experienced.

In the early church, it was always argued that *lex orandi* (the rule of worship), preceded *lex credendi* (the rule of faith or knowledge). I always remind my students in theology classes that the primitive Christian community first experienced the reality of God and salvation, then later, through reflection on that experience, developed their theology. In the modern world, we frequently reverse that order by teaching theology first and expecting experience and action to flow from this intellectual understanding. However, educators are now calling us back to the wisdom of the early church fathers. The argument that a person cannot know what he or she has not experienced is now widely received. For this reason a congregation that wants to evangelize and disciple new Christians must pay attention to its worship and teach the disciple how to have a relationship with God through worship.

What Does It Mean to Read and Pray the Scripture?

Third, the new convert learns *how to read and pray the Scripture*. Scripture, having been delivered to us by the inspiration of the Holy Spirit through the prophets and apostles, is the authoritative interpretation of God's saving events in history. It is the written text of the narrative the disciple has personally entered into in the church and thankfully remembers in worship. The congregation, the spiritual mentor, and the teacher of the small group must be aware of the shift that has recently taken place in the Christian attitude toward the Scripture. In modernity the Bible was read intellectually, in postmodernity the Bible is read spiritually.

Emphasis on the narrative structure of Scripture is the new approach to reading the Bible. It is not, as the liberals once said, a book about the human search to find God. Rather, it is a supernatural religious interpretation of the story of God and the world. It communicates that God created the world, that humanity rebelled against God, and that God became involved in history to rescue the world. The Hebrew Scriptures record God's involvement with Israel. The New Testament proclaims how God became incarnate in Jesus Christ, overcame the powers of evil through his death and resurrection, ascended into heaven, established the church as witness to the *Missio Dei,* until Christ returns to put away all evil and establish his rule over all the earth. It is in this narrative that the truth about life is revealed. The *hearer* needs to be taught how to read and listen to the Scripture for wisdom.

Wisdom comes from a spiritual reading of Scripture. Spiritual reading touches the heart, communicates to the inner person, and is God's voice given in a personal and relational way to those who read it in faith. The recovery of spiritual reading has taken the church back to an ancient method: *Lectio Divina* (divine reading). This method is used to disciple Christians into a *spiritual* rather than rationalistic way of embracing the Bible. Because the Bible is the word of God, the goal of *Lectio Divina* is union with God through a *meditative* and *contemplative* praying of Scripture. Through this form, the Word of God can take up residence within us and form us into the image of Christ. Thelma Hall, in *Too Deep for Words,* distinguishes between meditative and contemplative prayer:

> The word *meditation* refers to a discursive reading process in which words, events, etc., are prayerfully pondered and reflected on with the object of drawing from them some personal meaning or moral. It is basically an activity of the intellect and reason, aided by grace.
>
> *Contemplation* is variously described as a "resting" in God, or a "loving gaze" upon him, or a "knowing beyond knowing," or a "rapt attention" to God. All such attempts at verbalizing the experience necessarily fail to express the reality, for the simple reason that contemplation transcends the thinking and reasoning of meditation, as well as the emotions and "feelings" of the affective faculties. It is basically a prayer and experience of pure faith.[19]

Lectio Divina is primarily a subjective prayerful listening for the voice of God in Scripture. The monastic method of reading Scripture spiritually was captured by the medieval mystic Saint John of the Cross, who paraphrased Luke 11:19 into the four steps of *lectio*:

> Seek in READING
> And you will find in MEDITATION;
> Knock in PRAYER
> And it will be opened to you
> In CONTEMPLATION.[20]

To gain a better understanding of the method follow this procedure:

1. Read and listen to a text *(Lectio)*.
   Choose a text of Scripture to read slowly. *Listen* to the text with your heart and mind. *Hear* the Lord speaking to you in the text. Allow yourself to simply *be* with the text in an open and vulnerable way.
2. Reflect on the word *(Meditatio)*.
   By faith assume this text is *addressed to you*. Because God has "translated himself into our humanity, in Jesus," Jesus truly speaks to us by the spirit in a language we can understand. At the *meditatio* level it is important to ask, "What is it that you want me to hear?"
3. Let the word touch your heart (Prayer, *Oratio*).
   In *Oratio*, the word of God goes deeper into the self and becomes "the prayer of the heart." In this prayer open your heart so that his light may enter. The goal is like that of St. Augustine, who cried, "O God, our hearts are made for thee, and they shall be restless until they rest in thee." There emerges within the heart a "holy desire," a longing for the text, the word of God to be concretized in reality.
4. Enter into contemplation *(Contemplatio)*.
   Contemplatio shifts praying the Scripture into "a new language (silence)." This silence does not ask us to do anything, it is a call to *being*. Thomas Merton says, "The best way to pray is: stop! Let prayer pray within you, whether you know it or not."[21]

This fourfold process is described by a French Benedictine monk in the following way:

We read	*(Lectio)*
Under the eye of God	*(Meditatio)*
Until the heart is touched	*(Oratio)*
And leaps to flame	*(Contemplatio)*[22]

Lectio Divina does raise one question: What about the plurality of interpretations? Does this method of Scripture prayer lead us into a subjective relativism espoused by postmodern philosophy? Let me answer this question with a story.

Recently, I was discussing with a class this method of Scripture reading. One student told the following story that raised the crucial question of relativism for him: "I led my youth group in the study of a psalm," he said, "and then I asked, 'Did you hear God speak to you in the psalm?' One student said, 'Yes, God spoke to me in the phrase "and David sat down." God said to me through that phrase, "Your life is out of control, you need to take time to sit down, to relax, to be quiet." ' " My student asked, "How would you respond to this comment? That certainly isn't what the text means."

(Before I give my response, let it be said that my student was coming from the notion that the authorial intent of the writer is the only meaning of Scripture. This view puts the interpretation of Scripture into the hands of the scholar. In the end, we hear the voice of God through the scholar's interpretation. This method prevents relativistic interpretations of Scripture. But it is deadly. Is there a way to hear God's voice in Scripture and not be relativistic? Here's my answer:)

"Let your student have his interpretation," I said. "There is nothing in the phrase 'and David sat down' that contradicts either the universally accepted morality of Christianity or the universally affirmed teaching of the church."

These two matters are guidelines for hearing God in Scripture. If a person says, "I hear God saying Jesus is not God" or "Go and steal from your neighbor because he has an overabundance," you can be sure that is not the voice of God, for God has already spoken on matters of faith and morals in Scripture, and the church has arrived at an overwhelming consensus on these matters. If you hear "and David sat down" and, upon meditation and contemplation, you are moved to a less busy and more spiritually relaxed lifestyle, that is surely the voice of God for you in your present situation. Listen to God's voice, meditate on it, and let it pray within you (contemplation) and bring you to rest.

In sum, as you plan to implement the Worship, Evangelism, and Nurture Mission, do this: form the ministry teams of spiritual mentors and small group leaders. Then let them mentor the *hearer* into a personal relationship with the community, a participatory experience of worship, and an intimate relationship with God's Word as they learn how to pray the Scripture. In contrast to my opening example of Steve, who, left on his own after conversion, became a spiritual miscarriage, bring the new convert into the womb of a healthy church and provide intentional discipleship. This is what will keep the convert in the faith, in church, in worship, in Scripture.

9. The Rite of Covenant

The period of the *hearer* ends with a second passage rite—the symbol by which the disciple moves to an even deeper level of faith. In the early church it was called the rite of the enrollment of names (I have translated it as the rite of covenant). The emphasis is on God who has initiated a relationship and the *hearer* who has responded. We turn first to look at this rite in early church evangelism and then translate it into our contemporary situation.

The Rite of Covenant in the Early Church

According to Scripture, God always initiates a relationship. For example, God's choice of Israel to be his people is symbolized in a covenant ritual described in Exodus. The celebration of this ritual must have been an awesome moment for all of Israel. Imagine all the people gathered around the mountain in quiet expectancy. Then Moses stepped forth to act as mediator between the people and God. Reading the words of agreement between God and Israel, the people then responded "all the words that the LORD has spoken we will do" (Exod. 24:3). Then Moses, taking the blood of various sacrifices, threw half of the blood over the altar and half over the people in an act of ratification, saying, " 'See the blood of the covenant that the LORD has made with you in accordance with all these words' " (Exod. 24:8). In this ceremony, which must have trembled with an inexpressible mystery, a kind of rite of covenant was taking place. For here, at the foot of the mountain, Israel became the people of Yahweh and Yahweh became their God.

This theme of covenant permeates the New Testament as well. Paul reminded his readers at Ephesus that "he chose us in Christ before the foundation of the world . . . he destined us for adoption as his children through Jesus Christ" (Eph. 1:4-5). And Peter, writing to the Christians dispersed throughout the Roman Empire, referred to them as "chosen and destined by God the Father" (1 Pet. 1:2). In another passage Peter makes an obvious comparison of the people of the church to the people of Israel by describing the church as "chosen . . . , a royal priesthood, a holy nation, God's own people" (1 Pet. 2:9). As though to reinforce God's choice, Peter reminds these new Christians that "once you were not a people, but now you are God's people; once you had not received mercy, but now you have received mercy" (1 Pet. 2:10). In the early church, election was affirmed as a mystery. They had no theory. The new convert simply affirmed, "I have been called. God is doing a work in me. I am responding in faith."

Hippolytus describes the rite of covenant. "They who are to be set apart for baptism shall be chosen after their lives have been examined: whether they have lived soberly, whether they have honoured the widows, whether they have visited the sick, whether they have been active in well-doing. When their sponsors have testified that they have done these things, then let them hear the Gospel."[1]

Hippolytus indicates two essential parts to the rite of the covenant: the examination and the setting apart. The examination emphasized the style of life. The description of the examination stresses a sober life, caring for widows and the sick, and generally doing good to others. It sounds very similar to the summary of true religion given by James. "Religion that is pure and undefiled before God, the Father, is this: to care for orphans and widows in their distress, and to keep one-

117

self unstained by the world" (James 1:27). The examination provided an opportunity for the church to discern whether or not the conversion was authentic. To be authentic, the professed conversion had to result in a change of life. It was simply not enough to have a mere intellectual faith. Belief had to be accompanied by a change of life, habits, and orientation.

The role of the spiritual mentor is to testify to this change of life. The spiritual mentor, who may have brought the converting person as a seeker, stood with her at the rite of conversion (rite of welcome), and nurtured her through the *hearer* phase of growth, must now testify on her behalf in the rite of covenant. In the ancient church, the mentor was usually a friend, a relative, or a neighbor. In the third century, mentoring did not result from an institutional assignment but grew out of one-on-one evangelism. The mentor acted as a spiritual and personal guide through the conversion journey. Consequently, when the converting person was ready to take the final step toward baptism, the mentor testified to the seriousness of his or her commitment to the Christian faith and way of life.

The Rite of Covenant Today

The rite of covenant is considered a turning point in the process of spiritual formation. The convert has been in a period of discipleship. Now the church, upon the testimony of the mentor, receives the *hearer* into the final stage of spiritual preparation before baptism. Before the actual celebration of the rite of covenant, the disciple is examined in the areas of spiritual growth stressed during the hearer stage. This is done as an act of worship. This worship service, called the rite of covenant, consists of four parts:

(1) the presentation
(2) the examination

(3) admission

(4) prayer[2]

The rite is fairly brief and is usually conducted after the sermon. In the early church, this rite took place on the first Sunday of Lent.

The service for the rite of covenant is, of course, a moment of intense feeling not only for the disciple but also for the sponsors, relatives, and the whole Christian community. As in the ancient church, this rite has been designed to impress upon the *hearer* that he or she is here because of God's choosing. As God chose Abraham, Sarah, Moses, Miriam, David, Peter, Paul, John, and Mary Magdalene, so God chooses men and women to be members of his church.

The rite of covenant begins with the *presentation* of the *hearer* to the pastor. The presenter, one of the spiritual mentors or a small group leader, stands before the pastor and says something like this: "I present to you the people who have received Jesus Christ as their personal Savior. These people have been involved in the community, faithful in worship, and in the study of the Word. Now they wish to be baptized."

The pastor may say, "Those who are to be chosen by God to become full and active members of his church, please stand." The *hearers* stand together in a special place reserved for them. The pastor calls their name one by one. As each name is called, the hearer steps forward with the mentor and joins the group they will come to know so well. The pastor then asks the mentors to affirm that the *hearers* demonstrate new life in Christ.

The next part of the covenant is the *examination*. The pastors asks, "Do you wish to become a full member of God's church?" The disciple is then told, "As a sign of your commitment, write your name in the book." The disciple steps forward, takes the pen in hand, and writes his or her name in the book of covenant. This action expressed one more time the disciple's commitment to Christ and willingness to be baptized in his name.

Third, the pastor says the words of *admission*. The pastor explains that a signature in the book symbolizes that God knows the person, that God has chosen him or her, and that the person has responded with a yes. The pastor then turns to the mentor and reminds him or her that the responsibility toward the *hearer* is not over yet. The *hearer* is again entrusted to the mentor's care. The mentors are admonished to walk closely with the *hearer* the next several weeks as they prepare for baptism.

The covenant is completed with the *prayer*. The pastor asks the mentor to place a hand on the hearer's shoulder in the gesture of a caring relationship. The pastor then leads in prayer.

The covenant, like other rites, should not be taken lightly. Because of its emphasis—God has chosen you—it is an instrument of the Holy Spirit that shapes the experience of the convert. Consequently, it has the effect of drawing the *hearer* up into the message it proclaims, causing the *hearer* to participate in God's choosing not as a reluctant observer but as an active participant.

Suggestions on How to Do
the Rite of Covenant

- You will need a book for the enrollment of names.
- After the sermon, a person walks to the front bearing the book. This person proclaims to the pastor that the *hearers* have been studying in preparation for baptism (or reaffirmation of baptism in the event the person has been baptized). The leader opens the book and places it on a table.
- The pastor asks the *hearers* and their mentors to come and stand in a line near the table, with their mentors standing behind them. The mentors may place their hands on the *hearers'* shoulders or back.
- The pastor speaks to the *hearers*, reminding them that it is God who initiates a relationship and that God has called and chosen them to be in his church (Eph. 1:1-23).

1. THE EXPLANATION

- The pastor then addresses the *hearers* one-by-one or as a group, saying:

  "Do you once more affirm Jesus Christ as your Lord and Savior? If so, please write your name in this book as a sign of your faith."

2. THE ADMISSION

- The congregation looks on in silence as each *hearer* walks forward with his or her mentor to sign the book. After the signing, the mentor embraces the *hearer* with the sign of peace.
- After all of the *hearers* have enrolled their names the pastor turns to the congregation and says something like this:

  "I present to you the *hearers*. These *hearers* have been faithful in worship and in the study of the Word. They have proved themselves in the faith, in prayer, and in conduct. They will soon be baptized into the faith and brought into the full life of the church."

- The pastor addresses the *hearers* and now declares that they have moved to the *kneeler* phase of their spiritual process. The pastor welcomes them as *kneelers* and briefly describes *kneeler* time as an opportunity to learn the art of spiritual warfare.

The pastor closes with a prayer for the *kneelers'* spiritual formation.

In this section we have dealt with the formation of the new disciple. The aim of this time has been to emphasize the meaning of the church, its common worship, and commitment to reading and praying the Scripture. The period ends with the rite of covenant, one more opportunity to express faith in Jesus Christ as Lord and Savior. This passage rite is a significant milestone in the pilgrimage toward baptism and full participatory membership in the life of the church, for it deepens the hearers' commitment to Christ and the church, and readies them for the next stage of their journey—preparation for baptism.

Leader's Guide

A. EVALUATION
- What kind of "spiritual hero" image does this church project?
- Does this church create a "womb-like" atmosphere where new Christians can freely grow and thrive?
- How could this community better image what it means to be the church?
- Is the worship of this church spiritually engaging, or would you describe it with some other image?
- What does this church need to do to help people pray the scripture?

B. PLANNING A COURSE OF ACTION
   TO REVITALIZE THE CONGREGATION
- What do we need to do to better prepare this church to receive and form new Christians?
- What course of action should we take to disciple new Christians in the *hearer* phase?

C. PLANNING A COURSE OF ACTION FOR DISCIPLING THE HEARER

- Examine *Be My Disciple!* (Wheaton, Ill.: IWS Resources, 2001) for use in discipling new believers.
- Will your discipleship be best accomplished through a one-on-one relationship or a small group?
- What kind of training do you need to provide to the "spiritual mentor" and/or to the small-group leader?
- What are the intentional ways you make the *hearer* feel welcome in your midst?
- How will you develop and conduct the rite for the rite of covenant?

Resources for Further Reading

A resource for the hearer is *Be My Disciple!* (Wheaton, Ill.: IWS Resources, 2001). Suggested resources for leaders include Francis Kelly Nemeck and Marie Theresa Coombs, *The Way of Spiritual Direction* (Collegeville, Minn.: The Liturgical Press, 1985), a helpful guide for the spiritual mentor; Robert Wuthnow, *"I Come Away Stronger": How Small Groups Are Shaping American Religion* (Grand Rapids: Eerdmans, 1994); and Parker J. Palmer, *To Know as We Are Known: Education as Spiritual Journey* (San Francisco: HarperSanFrancisco, 1993), for the smaller-group leader; Stanley Hauerwas and William H. Willimon, *Resident Aliens: Life in the Christian Colony* (Nashville: Abingdon Press, 1989), for an understanding of the church; Robert E. Webber, *Worship Is a Verb: Eight Principles to Achieve Participatory Worship* (Peabody: Hendrickson, 1995), for the goal of achieving participatory worship; Thelma Hall, R. C., *Too Deep for Words: Rediscovering Lectio Divina* (New York: Paulist Press, 1988); and Gordon D. Fee and Douglas Stuart, *How to Read the Bible for All Its Worth: A Guide to Understanding the Bible*, 2d ed. (Grand Rapids: Zondervan, 1993), for teaching Scripture.

IV
Equipping the Kneeler

MENTORING THE
MATURE BELIEVER

JOURNEY TO JESUS

KNEELER

Spiritual Goal:
   Spiritual
   Formation
Passage Rite:
   Rite of Baptism
Resource:
   *Walk in the
   Spirit!*

INTRODUCTION

All of us struggle with the powers of evil that knock on our door and invite us to let them take up residence within us. But most of us are not willing to talk about the presence and influence of the powers of evil in our life.

Most of us are also probably unaware that there is an actual history of thinking through the various ways the powers draw us into their orbit. The sins that lurk inside us are not usually outright sins like murder, stealing, sexual unfaithfulness, blatant arrogance, or pride. Instead, our sins are more subtle, more nuanced, and perhaps even hidden from our own awareness.

I became aware of how subtle sin is in my own life when I first sought to do repentance (during Lent) using the St. Augustine prayer book. I was taken aback by the depth of the self-examination required by this exercise. It exposed within me the many hidden sins that lurk in the corners of my life.

During the period of spiritual formation the candidate must deal with the power of evil in the world and present in his or her life. The reality of evil and its influence is to be confronted during this period of spiritual growth.

10. Spiritual Formation in the Ancient Church

Spiritual Formation in the New Testament Church

In what some scholars have identified as prebaptismal instruction in the New Testament, Paul reminds his readers that "we are not contending against flesh and blood, but against the principalities, against the powers, against the world rulers of this present darkness, against the spiritual hosts of wickedness in the heavenly places" (Eph. 6:12 RSV).[1]

Paul's warning touches on a recurring theme in the primitive Christian community: the battle waged between the powers of evil and the power of Christ. When Adam and Eve chose evil over good, they initiated the contest between good and evil in human history. The writer of Genesis, capturing this dualism between the powers, predicts "enmity between you [Satan] and the woman, and between your seed and her seed; he shall bruise your head, and you shall bruise his heel" (Gen. 3:15 RSV).

This bitter struggle between good and evil is seen in the history of God's people, Israel. Even though they entered into covenant with God to become God's people, the powers of evil continually drew them away from this agreement. Israel's wandering in the wilderness for forty years was a prime example of their unfaithfulness. Forgetting the covenant, they turned to other gods. Even after entering into the promised land, they fell away from God again and again. The prophets momentarily brought them back, only to see Israel break covenant with God again.[2]

But the central conflict of the biblical story occurs in the life, death, and resurrection of Jesus Christ. For here is the account of how Satan bruised Christ's heel, and how Christ crushed the head of Satan. For example, Jesus frequently cast out demons from people (Mark 5:1-20) and claimed he could do so because he had entered into the domain of the wicked one and bound him (Matt. 12:29). In death, Christ "disarmed the principalities and powers and made a public example of them, triumphing over them in him" (Col. 2:15 RSV). Christ not only conquered the powers of evil in his death, but disarmed them so that they could no longer exercise ultimate control over his creatures and creation. In the resurrection, Jesus demonstrated his victory over the powers of death. "Death is swallowed up in victory" (1 Cor. 15:54 RSV)—no longer a power to be feared, no longer signifying the annihilation of human existence. Rather, because of Jesus' resurrection, the primitive Christian community was urged to break out into song. "Where, O death, is your victory? Where, O death, is your sting?" (1 Cor. 15:55).

Even the ascension of Jesus was understood by the primitive church in terms of the struggle between good and evil. For he ascended into heaven not to be absent from his people, but to sit at the right hand of power until all things have been put "under his feet" (see Eph. 1:21-23). Finally, the promise of the future is the final and ultimate destruction of Satan and all the powers of evil. In the end promises the Apocalypse, all powers of wickedness will be "thrown into the lake of fire and brimstone" (Rev. 20:10 RSV).

Christ, then, is the hero in the struggle between good and evil. He is the victor over sin, death, and the dominion of evil. But what about now? What about the time between the ascension and the consummation of history? Doesn't evil still exercise its influence over people, families, and nations? Isn't it still a power to be reckoned with?

The ancient church answered these questions in the affirmative. Nevertheless, the church fathers were convinced that the church had been appointed to witness to Christ's power, to proclaim "The universe is his!" and "Christ is victor!" Paul, for example, reminded the Ephesians that the victory of Christ over the powers is proclaimed to the world through the church. "Through the church the manifold wisdom of God might now be made known to the principalities and powers in the heavenly places" (Eph. 3:10 RSV). The church actively witnesses to the victory of God's redeeming power in a fallen world.

Furthermore, weapons of warfare have been given to the people of the church. "Put on the whole armor of God, that you may be able to stand against the wiles of the devil" (Eph. 6:11 RSV). Enumerating these weapons, Paul admonishes his readers to

> stand therefore, having girded your loins with truth, and having put on the breastplate of righteousness, and having shod your feet with the equipment of the gospel of peace; above all taking the shield of faith, with which you can quench all the flaming darts of the evil one. And take the helmet of salvation, and the sword of the Spirit, which is the word of God. Pray at all times in the Spirit, with all prayer and supplication. To that end keep alert with all perseverance, making supplication for all the saints. (Eph. 6:14-18 RSV)

This theme of battle with the powers of evil dominates the *kneeler* phase.[3] This phase checks the weapons and readies the warrior. Baptism into Christ is baptism into battle with the powers of evil. The battle is waged not alone, but with the company of God's people in the church. Therefore the *kneeler* learns how to draw on the spiritual resources that have been given to the church and to each member of the body of Christ.

The Kneeler Phase in the Ancient Church

In the third century, the person in the process of spiritual formation was called a *kneeler*. Even the name captures the shift to a deep personal spirituality. The former name of the converting person, *hearer*, implied standing, listening, taking it in, and knowing. But the name *kneeler* implies lowering the body and submitting. The *kneeler* stage is a new posture, a new growth, a new time for inner formation, for development and maturation into a new stage of being formed after Christ.

Kneeler time wrestles with the reality of evil. It deals with the constant attempt of the powers to pull the Christian away from new commitments, to drag the convert back into the service of the evil one. Consequently, the spiritual training of the *kneeler* focuses on this battle by admitting its reality and by providing the new Christian with spiritual resources with which to do battle with the temptations of the evil one. The *kneeler* is fortified spiritually by two specific spiritual actions: (1) prayers for cleansing, and (2) presentation of the Lord's Prayer and the creed as weapons of warfare.

Prayers for Cleansing

These prayers, which came to be known as the "scrutinies," required a complex set of actions, including prayer, anointings, and renunciations of Satan.[4] These prayers were spiritual and were not intended to examine a person's knowledge of the truth in intellectual terms. They had to do with disposition, intention, purpose, and orientation. They related to the heart's battle with lust, greed, envy, anger, hatred, and the like. They expressed the conflict that all God's people have with the lure of evil and the temptation to pursue the world, the flesh, and the devil. Augustine defined the role of both the church and the candidates in these prayers. "We heap upon the head of your enemy all the anathemas which his heinous crimes deserve. On your part, give yourselves completely to this glorious battle, so that with the proper horror you may renounce all your contacts with him."[5] On three Sundays during Lent, the *kneelers* came to the front of the community to receive prayer on their behalf.

There were also *daily prayers* that occurred on the six days of Holy Week before the baptism. They culminated in the bishop's prayer and in the *rite of breathing*. According to Hippolytus, the bishop would have "his hand upon them . . . shall exorcise [pray] all evil spirits to flee away and never to return; when he has done this he shall breathe in their faces, seal their foreheads, ears and noses, and then raise them up."[6]

The tradition of *breathing* in the face of the candidate relates to the ancient understanding of the Holy Spirit. It rests on the belief that when God created Adam and "breathed into his nostrils the breath of life" (Gen. 2:7 RSV), it was the Holy Spirit that Adam received. When Adam and Eve fell away from God, they lost the presence of the Holy Spirit in their lives and in the lives of their descendants. But now, in conversion, the Holy Spirit is given back again. Consequently, the prayers and the rite of breathing are closely related, for as the prayer calls for the convert to be rid of the spirit of evil, the breath symbolizes the new infusion of the Holy Spirit.

A third rite, that of *sealing* the candidate with the sign of the cross on the forehead, ears, and nose complements the prayers and breathing, because it symbolizes the promise of salvation that comes from the unfailing love of God. Together, these three rites point to the meaning of the *kneeler* period—they symbolize the movement from the clutches of the evil one to life in the Spirit. Here, for example, is a sample prayer from the fourth century:

> *The Scrutiny takes place in the church in the presence of all the clergy and faithful.*
> *The candidates come forward for the exorcisms at the deacon's summons. Barefoot and dressed only in penitents' tunics,*

they stand on sackcloth with bowed heads, while the bishop prays:

God of Abraham, God of Isaac, and God of Jacob,
You are the God who appeared to Your servant Moses on
   Mount Sinai,
the God who led Israel out of Egypt.
In Your mercy You appointed an angel to guard them
   day and night.
We ask You now, Lord,
to send Your holy angels to these servants of Yours also,
and bring them to the grace of baptism.

The deacon instructs their sponsors to make the sign of the cross on the foreheads of their . . . [children]. One of the exorcists then lays his hands on each of them in turn, saying in a loud voice:

Remember, you accursed, devil,
the sentence that was passed upon you,
and give honor to the living and true God!
Give honor to Jesus Christ His Son,
and to the Holy Spirit,
and depart from these servants of God
whom our Lord Jesus Christ has called
to receive His holy grace and blessing
in the waters of baptism.
We adjure you, cursed devil,
never dare to violate it!

An acolyte makes the sign of the cross on the foreheads of the candidates. Then a second exorcist lays his hands on them, and says:

Hear this, you cursed devil!
I command you in the name of the eternal God
and of our Savior Jesus Christ
to depart in confusion,
a victim of your own envy.

You no longer have anything in common with these
   servants of God;
their thoughts are already turned toward heavenly
   things.
They are ready to renounce you and the world
   in order to live the blessed life of immortality.
Give honor, therefore,
to the Holy Spirit who is about to come upon them.
May He descend from heaven,
cleanse and hallow them in the sacred font,
and make their hearts the temple and dwelling place of God.
So shall these servants of God,
freed from all stain of past sin,
give thanks to God without ceasing
and bless His holy name for ever,
through Christ our Lord.

All respond: AMEN.
The signing and laying on of hands are repeated for the third
time, with the following words:

I exorcise you, unclean spirit,
in the name of the Father,
and of the Son,
and of the Holy Spirit,
and command you to come out of these servants of God.
Depart from them, cursed fiend!
He who commands you is the one who walked on the
   sea
and stretched out His hand to Peter
when he was about to sink.
He who commands you is the one
who opened the eyes of the man born blind,
and raised Lazarus to life
after he had been in the grave four days.
Remember then that you are damned,
and give honor to the living and true God,
to Jesus Christ His Son,
and to the Holy Spirit.

Finally one of the priests marks the candidates' foreheads with the sign of the cross, lays his hands on their head and prays:

O Lord most holy,
Almighty Father and Eternal God,
the Author of light and truth,
I ask Your everlasting mercy
on behalf of these servants of Yours.
Enlighten them with knowledge of Yourself;
cleanse and sanctify them;
give them true wisdom;
make them worthy to receive the grace of baptism,
and help them to persevere
in firm hope,
an upright will,
and sound faith,
through Christ our Lord.[7]

All respond: AMEN.

This prayer reflects the particular language of the fourth century. Its content and spirit may be retained in a language more common to the twenty-first century.

The Presentations of the Creed and the Lord's Prayer

During this phase of spiritual formation, the *kneeler* is presented the Apostles' Creed and the Lord's Prayer. The prayers called for the purification of the *kneeler,* and the presentations symbolized a deeper understanding of the faith. In special ceremonies, the kneelers received the creed (an early form of the Apostles' Creed) and the Lord's Prayer, which embody the church's tradition of faith and prayer. Like the prayers, the presentations are not to be seen as symbols of a mere intellectual Christianity. Rather, they are symbols of the weapons used by Christians for their warfare against the power of evil.

In the ancient church, the creed was delivered orally, and *kneelers* were required to memorize it verbatim. Handing the creed down orally rather than in written form emphasized its living power in a person's life as opposed to being only an objective, intellectual statement of faith. For example, Cyril of Jerusalem, who was well known for his catechetical lectures delivered in the Church of the Holy Sepulchre, told the candidate to memorize the creed and to "keep this faith as the only provision you need for your journey all the rest of your life, and receive no other."[8] As this example shows, the creed is delivered to the candidate as food, sustenance, and nourishment. It feeds the soul, strengthens the heart, and aids the convert in the battle with the powers of evil. It defines the Christian's place in the world and permeates the whole of his or her actions. Augustine captured this spirit of the creed by telling new converts that "it will be written in your hearts, so that you may love what you believe and that, through love, faith may work in you and that you may become pleasing to the Lord God."[9]

This goal is illustrated in *Egira's Travel*. According to Egira, the instructor taught the creed during Lent, phrase by phrase, explaining both its literal and spiritual meaning. Then, at the end of Lent, the bishop's chair was placed behind the altar. When the bishop sat in his seat, the candidates for baptism came one-by-one and recited the creed from memory.[10]

The Lord's Prayer was also committed to memory. While the *kneeler* had already been taught to pray, the Lord's Prayer was reserved for baptized Christians, as in the spirit of Augustine: "How can someone say 'Our Father' if he has not yet been born."[11] The emphasis placed on this prayer by the early church fathers had to do not only with what the convert wanted from the Father but what the candidate for baptism ought to have wanted. Specifically, what the *kneeler* ought to have wanted was for God's will to be done in his or her life as God's will was done on earth.

Both of these rituals—the creed and the Lord's Prayer—embody what theologian Michael Dujarier calls "the formulas which have carried the Church's traditions of faith and of prayer from one generation of believers to the next."[12] Perhaps we can assume that when the candidates received the creed and the Lord's Prayer, they knew they were being entrusted with the heart of the gospel. They knew they were soon to be baptized into this truth and an approach to life that they had been learning for several years.

Conclusion

The *kneeler* period emphasizes spiritual recollection and readiness. It brings before the convert the essence of what it means to be in Christ, and equips the *kneeler* with the weapons of spiritual warfare. It calls the *kneeler* into an ultimate rejection of Satan and all works of evil. It bids the *kneeler* to receive the tradition of faith and prayer that has been handed down in the church from the beginnings of Christianity. To reject Satan and accept the tradition deepen faith and provide the *kneeler* with one more opportunity to express his or her commitment to Jesus Christ as Lord and Savior.

11. Spiritual Formation Today

The *kneeler* stage is quite different from either the *seeker* or *hearer* stage, and differentiation must be noted. The goal of the *seeker* phase is conversion. It is a beginning in the Christian faith, the first act of coming into the church, as the rite of conversion symbolizes. The goal of the *hearer* phase is to solidify conversion by becoming a disciple. The *hearer* phase emphasizes the way of doing. It says the Christian has a new life—a new community, and a new narrative by which to live, a book to guide him or her in all matters of faith and practice. The *kneeler* phase takes the disciple one step deeper because it has to do with the formation of the inner self, the way of being. It says that being a spiritual person and following after Jesus is a day-by-day battle with the powers of evil. It says you don't do it alone; you stay on course with Jesus strengthened by the prayers of the church, the faith of the church, and your own personal prayer. This is the formation of the inner self, a special kind of discipline. Joseph Allen, in *Inner Way*, writes of this journey:

> To enter the *inner way* is risky, dangerous—one can even say "fearful." There are a multitude of reasons why this is so. Most of all, it is fearful because it represents an encounter of spiritual depth, one which not only leads to a deeper relationship among human persons, but also seeks to carry us to the very root of all relationships—the presence of the living God himself. In the *inner way* one learns what the scripture means: "It is a fearful thing to fall into the hands of the living God." (Heb. 10:31)[1]

The goal of this phase of the journey is to bring the *kneeler* into a deeper spirituality through teaching spiritual warfare, learning how to pray, and embracing the Apostles' Creed.

Teaching Spiritual Warfare

We live a neo-pagan world that bears striking similarities to that of the third century. Today, the church must take into consideration three competing realities:

(1) We live in a time of the *breakdown of Christian values.* Values of personal morality and Christian virtue have been lost.[2]
(2) We live in a time when *secular values of the American dream and of capitalism have been christianized.* Ambition, success, thrift, wealth, being nice, dressing right, and playing the political game are exonerated as characteristics of "good" Christians.
(3) This paradox of the loss of Christian values and the contrasting christianization of secular values is further complicated by the *emergence of numerous New Age Eastern religions and other non-Christian spiritualities.* Furthermore, Christian spirituality must be forged out in a world that values plurality and scorns assertions of truth.

How do we teach spirituality in this context? First, spirituality means to *trust in Jesus* as the only one who can restore our relationship to the Father. Through trust we are in union with Jesus, and through Jesus we are united to the Father. Therefore we have a calling to have faith in Jesus and to grow into his image of true humanity. Once this kind of spirituality has been grasped, we can agree with Eugene Peterson, who writes: "The Christian life . . . is a recovery of what was lost at the fall";[3] or with Ranald Macaulay and Jerram Barrs, who write: "The whole purpose of the Christian life is the recovery of the original image of God";[4] or with Dallas Willard, who writes: "We can become like Christ by doing one thing—by following him in the overall style of life he chose for himself."[5] But how can we accomplish this goal?

The goal of "humanity restored" is already accomplished by Jesus. In the incarnation God was united with humanity. In Jesus, perfect divinity and perfect humanity are united. Jesus lifts humanity, through faith, into a relationship with the divine. By faith we are in Christ. He represents us to the Father. In him we are, as Martin Luther said, "saints." On the other hand, in this world we are not yet perfect. We are, as Luther said, "sinners." Thus spirituality is what we are becoming while still in this world. Our calling is to become truly human, to experience a repair of the brokenness of our humanity and to reach out toward that new restored humanity, which we are in Christ. This is our calling, to "throw off everything that hinders and the sin that so easily entangles, and let us run with perseverance the race marked out for us" (Heb. 12:1 NIV). It is a long obedience in the same direction,[6] obedience rooted in the conflict with evil on the one hand, and the freedom we have in Christ on the other hand.

Second, spirituality has to do with *how we handle the conflict* between good and evil. The powers of evil will not give up, even though they have been defeated. Individuals continue to raise the fist of rebellion against God. These powers of evil will continue to knock on the doors of the hearts and minds of Christians, continually tempting them to turn back to sin instead of choosing to live in the freedom of their new nature. Paul, the chief of the apostles, acknowledged this struggle: "I find this law at work: When I want to do good, evil is right there with me" (Rom. 7:21 NIV).

Christian spirituality acknowledges the tension between what we are and what we have been called to become. We are all engaged in a spiritual warfare.[7] We are sinners, broken vessels of humanity, called in Christ who has rescued us to become more and more like Jesus. The New

Testament continually presents this tension as the conflict in which we engage to become whole, to achieve what it means to be a redeemed and rescued human. In Romans 6 we are told: "Count yourselves dead to sin but alive to God in Christ Jesus" (v. 11 NIV); In Romans 7: "In my inner being I delight in God's law; but I see another law at work in the members of my body, waging war against the law of my mind and making me a prisoner of the law of sin at work within my members (vv. 22-23 NIV). In Romans 8, the presentation of the conflict continues: "If you live according to the sinful nature, you will die; but if by the Spirit you put to death the misdeeds of the body, you will live (v. 13 NIV). This theme of battle is continued through the other Epistles as well:

> Put to death, therefore, whatever belongs to your earthly nature: sexual immorality, impurity, lust, evil desires and greed . . . rid yourselves of all such things as these: anger, rage, malice, slander, and filthy language from your lips. Do not lie to each other . . . put on the new self, which is being renewed in knowledge in the image of its Creator . . . clothe yourselves with compassion, kindness, humility, gentleness and patience. . . . Forgive as the Lord forgave you. And over all these virtues put on love . . . Let the peace of Christ rule in your hearts . . . be thankful. Let the word of Christ dwell in you richly . . . sing psalms, hymns and spiritual songs with gratitude in your hearts . . . whatever you do, . . . do it all in the name of the Lord Jesus. (Col. 3:5-17 NIV)

These passages and many more throughout the New Testament have been identified by scholarship as possible prebaptismal instruction. They all have to do with the human condition, with how the believer once lived and how the Christian has been born into a new life. A pointed example is Galatians 5:16-26. More than likely this list of vices and virtues was available to the community before Paul penned the letter to the Galatians. Paul is mindful of how the Galatians had fallen away from their original commitment to Christ. He opens his letter to them by saying, "I am astonished that you are so quickly deserting the one who called you" (1:6 NIV). He is referring to how they put themselves back under the law in the hope of attaining salvation by works (3:1-5). But Paul, using their own prebaptismal creed, calls them back to freedom (5:1-15). His message is that their attempt to save themselves by keeping the law has put them back under the law. He reminds them how their prebaptismal instruction taught that to be in Christ is to live in the freedom of the Spirit. Paul reminds them of what they have become free *from* and what they have become free *to*. Here is a summary in chart form to emphasize that true spirituality is to "put off" and "put on."

PUT OFF: Acts of the sinful nature	PUT ON: The fruit of the Spirit
sexual immorality impurity debauchery idolatry witchcraft hatred discord jealousy fits of rage selfish ambition dissensions factions envy drunkenness orgies	love joy peace patience kindness goodness faithfulness gentleness self-control

This sense of conflict and the call to choose the good continue to be found in the baptismal literature of the early church. The *Didache* is a good example. This noncanonical book may have been written as early as A.D. 50 and probably no later than A.D. 120. Its first six chapters constitute prebaptism training in spirituality and concentrate on what the writer calls "the two ways." Here are some timely excerpts from this ancient document:

> "Do not murder; do not commit adultery"; do not corrupt boys; do not fornicate; "do not steal"; do not practice magic; do not go in for sorcery; do not murder a child by abortion or kill a new-born infant. "Do not covet your neighbor's property; do not commit perjury; do not bear false witness"; do not slander; do not bear grudges. Do not be double-minded or double-tongued, for a double tongue is "a deadly snare." Your words shall not be dishonest or hollow, but substantiated by action. Do not be greedy or extortionate or hypocritical or malicious or arrogant. Do not plot against your neighbor. Do not hate anybody; but reprove some, pray for others, and still others love more than your own life.
>
> My child, flee from all wickedness and from everything of that sort. Do not be irritable, for anger leads to murder. Do not be jealous or contentious or impetuous, for all this breeds murder.
>
> My child, do not be lustful, for lust leads to fornication. Do not use foul language or leer, for all this breeds adultery.
>
> My child, do not be a diviner, for that leads to idolatry. Do not be an enchanter or an astrologer or a magician. Moreover, have no wish to observe or heed such practices, for all this breeds idolatry.
>
> My child, do not be a liar, for lying leads to theft. Do not be avaricious or vain, for all this breeds thievery.
>
> My child, do not be a grumbler, for grumbling leads to blasphemy. Do not be stubborn or evil-minded, for all this breeds blasphemy.
>
> But be humble since "the humble will inherit the earth."

Be patient, merciful, harmless, quiet, and good; and always "have respect for the teaching" you have been given. Do not put on airs or give yourself up to presumptuousness. Do not associate with the high and mighty; but be with the upright and humble. Accept whatever happens to you as good, in the realization that nothing occurs apart from God. . . .

Those who persecute good people, who hate truth, who love lies, who are ignorant of the reward of uprightness, who do not "abide by goodness" or justice, and are on the alert not for goodness but for evil: gentleness and patience are remote from them. "They love vanity," "look for profit," have no pity for the poor, do not exert themselves for the oppressed, ignore their Maker, "murder children," corrupt God's image, turn their backs on the needy, oppress the afflicted, defend the rich, unjustly condemn the poor, and are thoroughly wicked. My children, may you be saved from all this!

See "that no one leads you astray" from this way of the teaching, since such a one's teaching is godless.[8]

In sum, the *kneeler* phase teaches that Christian spirituality is in Jesus. We are spiritual because of our union by faith in him. Therefore we are called to be like Jesus—living in the pattern of his death and resurrection—dying to sin and being resurrected to the fruit of the Spirit. But that is not all. We are also members of the community of Jesus and the church, and are fortified by the prayers of the church, by the creed, and by the Lord's Prayer. These are the means by which the *kneeler* is formed as a spiritual person.

Prayers for the Kneeler

First, the spirituality of the *kneeler* is formed by the prayers of the church. For at least three Sundays during worship, the candidates for baptism are called to come forward for prayer.

The prayers may be conducted right after the sermon or

at some other appropriate time. The *kneelers* are invited to stand with their mentors in the front of the church. The leader of worship invites the congregation to pray that the *kneeler* may be characterized by a spirit of repentance, and a knowledge of their acceptance by God.

During the prayer, the mentor places a hand on the shoulder of the *kneeler*. The leader prays for special intentions such as that the kneelers "may keep the Word of God in their hearts," or that "they may learn to know Christ," and that "they may sincerely reject anything in their lives which is displeasing to Christ or opposed to him."[9]

In the closing prayer, the pastor asks all the *kneelers* to join hands. The prayer consists of intercessions such as "never let the powers of evil deceive them" and "free them from the spirit of falsehood." If time permits, hands are laid upon each individual, with a particular brief prayer for that person. The prayer concludes with a prayer to Jesus. The pastor and people extend their hands over the *kneelers* and call upon Jesus to display his love in each person.

Throughout its history, the church has developed prayer for the putting off of vices and the attainment of virtues. These prayers have nourished Christians into spiritual growth toward the riches of becoming more fully human. There has been a resurgence of these prayers in past decades and new opportunities to draw on the great spiritual traditions of the past.

The Apostles' Creed

Second, the *kneelers'* spirituality is strengthened by the faith of the Apostles' Creed, the summary of faith. The early church chose the creed to be a symbol of spirituality because they knew the Christian faith had to do with the formation of the mind. The church was cognizant of Paul's injunction: "Be transformed by the renewing of your minds" (Rom. 12:2).

Current educational theories recognize the importance

and the validity of cognitive development.[10] One of the main theories affirms that development occurs through the transformation of the cognitive structure. The Apostles' Creed is a cognitive worldview that is not attained by a social process, but by a conversion to a new way of seeing reality. In this sense, the creed is an intellectual commentary on the Christian narrative. It affirms the Trinity and trinitarian action in the world through the Father who creates, the Son who becomes incarnate, and the Spirit who now works in the world and in the church. The new convert accepts this worldview, not out of reason, but out of a conversion. A second theory of cognitive development is that growth occurs in interacting with other people. This principle points to instruction exchanged between small groups, or between the mentor and the new believer. The creed represents the historic tradition of the church handed down from one generation to another. The creed must be explained to the new believer who has entered into this worldview through conversion. A third insight suggests that cognitive development takes place in a sequence of stages. In the Worship, Evangelism, and Nurture Mission, the cognitive stage is not the first priority, but commitment and then development of the disciples' minds. Cognitive commitments are made in the process of theological reflection on faith that has been embraced. In all this we see that one must believe in order to know.

Reflection on the creed during the *kneeler* phase is an essential part of Christian nurture. Baptism is into Christ and the faith of the church about Christ. In a society of New Age spirituality, in which it is common to say "I believe in Jesus," it is necessary to define what is meant by that phrase. The Apostles' Creed is a summary of Christian faith that clarifies what we mean by faith in Jesus: the creed witnesses to who Jesus is in the community of the Godhead; the creed connects the *kneeler* to Christians of the past as well as all those who globally confess Jesus; and the creed is a protection against a distorted view of Christianity. Here is a reconstruction of the early church's instruction on the creed:

> By this faith we know that there is one God, the source of all things, who made everything out of nothing. By this faith we know that the dead will rise again. By faith we know that the Father has a Son who shares His own nature. By faith we know that the Holy Spirit is God and that He is the Spirit of Father and Son. By faith we are convinced of the truth of the saving plan by which God the Son became incarnate in our world. . . .
>
> The creed is part of your Christian armor. It is a provision for your journey that you must retain as long as your life lasts. Never accept any other faith than this, not even if I should change my mind and say something that contradicts what you are now being taught; no, not if the spirit of darkness were to disguise himself as an angel of light and lead you astray. Guard it with the utmost care, or the old enemy will seize his chance to ruin you by tempting you to prefer your own notions to the teaching of the Church, or else some false Christian will deceive you by misrepresenting the truths that have been handed on to you. Faith, you might say, is like cash paid over the counter. I am handing over the cash to you now, but God will require an account from you of what you have received.
>
> Remember what Saint Paul says to Timothy: "I charge you before God, who gives life to all, and before Jesus Christ who gave testimony before Pontius Pilate, to keep this faith that is committed to you spotless until our Lord Jesus Christ appears. A treasure of life has been entrusted to you, and at His coming the Master will look for the deposit." (1 Tim. 5:21; 6:13-15)[11]

The Lord's Prayer

Third, the spirituality of the *kneeler* is fortified through personal prayer. In prayer, we respond to the world, suffering, dying, rejoicing, growing, sinning, and being blessed. But we respond to the world through the One in whom the world is truly seen—the One who always points us in the same direction the divine love looks . . . [W]e uncover the kind of holiness which being in the world with Jesus requires. The deep emotions of gratitude, repentance, and joy, the virtues of humility, hope, and compassion in solidarity with all human beings, indeed with all creatures—these are the human realities which are the bloodstream of prayer. . . . We are to signify Christ to the world, even as Christ is given to us continually in our praying through him.[12]

This unity between prayer and doctrine, prayer and life, prayer and the affections, prayer and the virtues seems to coincide with prayer in the ancient church. Prayer is not a mere assertion of wants or needs, but of union with God and with the purposes of God in the world. Perhaps that is why the Lord's Prayer is memorized by the *kneeler* and presented as armor against all that is sin and death. Praying the Lord's Prayer is to enter into union with Jesus and with his purposes here in history. The structure of the prayer is itself instructive, for it covers the whole extent of the prayer life. First, three petitions are directed toward God. Each one proclaims how God may be glorified:

- Hallowed be thy name
- Thy kingdom come
- Thy will be done on earth as it is in heaven

Second, four petitions have to do with God's people:

- Give us this day our daily bread
- Forgive us our trespasses as we forgive those who trespass against us
- And lead us not into temptation
- But deliver us from evil

Third, the prayer ends with a doxological affirmation of faith.

- For thine is the kingdom and the power and the glory forever and ever. Amen.

Dallas Willard puts the Lord's Prayer into perspective: "It is an enduring framework for all praying. You only move beyond it provided you stay within it. . . . It is a powerful lens through which one constantly sees the world as God himself sees it."[13] Once again, as in all aspects of the Christian faith, being in a faithful prayer relationship with God means to live *within* the narrative of God's doing. Prayer is to be in harmony with God's mission for the world—the overcoming of the evil powers, and the rescue of all creation for God.

The Presentations

Finally, in today's symbol-oriented world, the significance for Christian knowledge and prayer are accented for the *kneeler* in the presentations. The church needs to have a special Sunday morning ceremony before the baptism, presenting the *kneeler* with a copy of the creed[14] and the Lord's Prayer,[15] with an admonition to live daily in faith and prayer. This ceremony impresses the *kneeler* and the congregation with the power of faith and prayer against the enemy of the gospel—the principalities and the powers.

Conclusion

The twenty-first century may seem worlds apart from the third and fourth centuries. However, the spirit of the contemporary age does not differ vastly from the pagan era of antiquity. In our time of secularization, materialism, sensualism, and violence, the need to be aware of the principalities and powers that pull us into the evils of the day is every bit as urgent as it has been in the past. Consequently, the formation of the *kneeler* maintains the spirit of the early church.

The *kneeler* period is a time for reflection, a time to enter the desert and be alone, a time to prepare for baptism. The image of an arid, lifeless desert conveys the power of evil to destroy God's creation, to spoil it, and to turn it into a wasteland. Here God's people wrestle with the power of evil before moving on to proclaim God's power over evil. Moses, the prophets, John the Baptist, Jesus, Paul, and, after them, the hermits of the early church went to the desert, not to escape temptation, but to confront it and to overcome it.[16] In the desert, the *kneeler* wrestles once more with the demons that would draw them toward evil, a process that is at the heart of conversion. They conquer those demons in the name of Jesus and adorn themselves with the Holy Spirit. The prayers and presentations help the convert to recollect his or her spiritual journey and assist him or her in moving more deeply into the life of the Holy Spirit.

Imagine that you have gone through the entire process of conversion, you are deeply committed to the faith and to prayer, and are now anxiously awaiting the day of your baptism. Here you are, perhaps on the last Sunday of Lent, now standing before the minister in the presence of the congregation you have come to love as your extended family. The minister says, "My dear friends, listen carefully to the words of that faith by which you are to be justified. The words are few, but the mysteries they contain are awe-inspiring. Accept them with a sincere heart and be faithful to them." Then, following the lead of the minister, you recite from memory the Apostles' Creed, savoring every phrase, every word. For here is something more than a statement of faith, it is a credo of life, a commitment from which you view and live all of life. Then, in this or another service of worship, you are given the rule of prayer. You are invited to say the Lord's Prayer, not just as words, but as the fundamental commitment of your life. With each phrase and word, you recall the instruction and values that you received and by which you now live.

The recitation of the creed and the Lord's Prayer are not simply formalities. They deal with the very essence of that tradition that reaches back through history to the time of Christ and his disciples. What they believed and taught has been handed down from generation to generation in the church. Now, almost two thousand years after the event, the candidate accepts that tradition with the spiritual intent and meaning that countless millions of people throughout history have experienced. This is no dry, rote action. It trembles with an inexpressible mystery, immerses us in the meaning of faith, and penetrates into our very being, bringing us into the narrative of history and salvation as participants with firsthand experience.

12. The Rite of Baptism

I grew up in the home of a Baptist pastor where adult baptism was the norm. As an infant, I was dedicated in the arms of my parents. While this dedication differed from infant baptism in that water was not used, it was similar in that it called upon God to choose me as his own, and it placed upon my parents and the congregation the duty of bringing me up in the faith.

I was baptized as a teenager. Although it was a simple baptism, it contained some basic symbols that I have never forgotten. For example, baptism was treated as a necessary aspect of my converting process. It was not an option depending on my whim or fancy. I was aware that if I refused to be baptized, I would in effect be rejecting the faith. I recognized that my choice to be baptized was a sign of my acceptance of the faith.

Several simple symbols of my baptism have their roots in the ancient church. The primary symbol was immersion in water in the name of Jesus Christ. This action symbolized my burial with Christ and my resurrection with him from the tomb. Three other symbols, which were secondary but still of great importance, were the robing, the renunciation, and the affirmation. I was dressed in white robes to signify my new relationship to Christ. Then, while in the water, I was asked, "Do you renounce Satan and all his works?" To which I answered, "I do." And, finally, after the renunciation I was asked, "Do you receive Jesus Christ as your Lord and Savior?" To which I answered, "I do." I was unaware that these three symbols originated in the primitive Christian community, but I did sense the powerful meaning they contained. The baptismal ceremony, simple as it was made a lasting impression upon me. To this day when I am asked to give testimony of my faith, I always go back to my baptism as the turning point of my personal experience with Christ.

Baptism in the New Testament

The New Testament contains a considerable number of stories and allusions to baptism. These passages reveal the roots of the meaning of baptism and the origins of later symbolic ceremonies. Baptism in the primitive Christian community clearly had a twofold meaning: it identified the convert with the death and resurrection of Christ and brought the convert into a new relationship with the church. For example, the convert was seen as the recipient of the work of Jesus. The convert was "baptized into his death" in order to "walk in newness of life." The impact of baptism was "that our old self was crucified with him so that the body of sin might be destroyed, and we might no longer be enslaved to sin" (Rom. 6:6). Here baptism is seen as a turning point, the event that marks the convert's turning away from the powers of evil toward the kingdom of Christ. But this is only made possible because of what Christ has done. He has defeated the powers of sin and death in his own death and resurrection. The result of this victory is then passed on to the convert through baptism.

Baptism also brings the convert into a new community of people, the church. Baptism is never portrayed in the New Testament as individualistic salvation. It is always salvation into a new society of people, the body of Christ. In the description of the earliest Christian conversions, the converts were "added" to the church (Acts 2:41). This implies that they did not start a new church but were included in the one church, the one body of Christ that had already been formed. Thirty years later, Paul wrote to the Corinthians and reminded them that "in one spirit we were all baptized into one body—Jews or Greeks, slaves or free—and we were all made to drink of one Spirit" (1 Cor. 12:13).

From these two meanings of baptism—participation in Christ and entering the community of faith—the New Testament church developed a number of symbols to convey the meaning of baptism in action as well as in words. Those New Testament sources may be organized into three categories:

(1) *rites* that proclaim the meaning of baptism
(2) *images* of baptism from the Old Testament
(3) *symbols* that relate to the reception of the Holy Spirit

First, we have inherited many rites that relate to the meaning of baptism. For example, baptism begins with the apostolic proclamation of salvation through Christ. But, as we have seen, the pagan situation of the early church made it necessary to instruct converts before baptism. They were instructed in faith and morals. For example, Paul speaks of the necessity of believing in one God (1 Thess. 1:9). This may account for the development of the study of the creed. Second, Paul refers to the moral standards of the faith (Rom. 6:17). This may account for the prebaptismal emphasis on a way of life (see Gal. 5:16-25). The Gentiles were polytheistic and amoral. They needed instruction in faith and morals. This need probably stands behind the development of the seven-step process.

Rites were also created to symbolize "putting on" the new life in Christ. The major rites of transition, such as the rite of welcome, the enrollment of names, and the rites of baptism, symbolize this New Testament idea. In baptism rites such as disrobing before baptism and putting on the new white robe after baptism capture the essence of Paul's instruction, that in conversion and baptism we "put off" the old man and "put on" the new man (Col. 3:1-17). The idea of transference from one kingdom to another can also be traced to the New Testament baptismal hymns, which celebrate crossing over into the kingdom of Christ. Finally, the most essential aspect of baptism—the immersion in water in the name of the Father, Son, and Holy Spirit—conveys the concept of transition, for it symbolizes burial into Christ's death and a rising to new spiritual life through his resurrection.

Second, the New Testament contains images of baptism from the Old Testament. For example, baptism is compared to the crossing of the Red Sea by the Israelites (1 Cor. 10:1-2). The manna/Eucharist typology is employed in John 6. Next, circumcision is seen as a stripping away of the old flesh (Col. 2:11-12). Finally, a number of allusions refer to the new birth (John 2:3-5, Titus 3:5; and 1 Pet. 1:3; 2:2.). These images not only provide the source for later ceremonial developments in baptism but also imply that ceremonial actions already accompanied baptism in the New Testament community.

Third, baptism is full of symbols that express the reception of the Holy Spirit. Paul writes: "You were washed, you were sanctified, you were justified in the name of the Lord Jesus Christ and in the Spirit of our God" (1 Cor. 6:11). The laying on of hands (Acts 8; Acts 9; Heb. 6:2) is a rich gesture that symbolizes the gift of the Holy Spirit. These images inform the latter rite of anointing with oil to symbolize the gift of the Holy Spirit in the life of the new believer.

Baptism in the ancient church develops in keeping with its primitive meaning and roots, enriched by actions that convey the meaning of conversion into Christ and the church.

Baptism in the Ancient Church

During the mid–second century, Justin Martyr described the basic structure of ancient baptism. According to Justin, baptism consists of three parts:

(1) preparation before Easter
(2) the baptism itself
(3) the first eucharistic celebration with the whole community[1]

For more insight into these parts, let us turn to *The Apostolic Tradition of Hippolytus.*

First, the baptisms occurred on *Easter Sunday.*[2] The candidates for baptism fasted from Friday until Sunday. On Saturday they went to the church for a prayer of exorcism, which was followed by the sign of the cross over each of the senses, signifying the conversion of the whole person. Next, the candidates attended an all-night (Saturday) vigil, listening to readings and instruction concerning baptism and the new life in Christ. They were then baptized early in the morning of Easter, signifying their union with Christ.

A second feature of baptism in the early church was *immersion in water.*[3] From the very beginning of Christian baptism, water has been one of the major symbols of new birth. While water does symbolize washing and cleansing, its central symbol is its power to create. The fathers of the church point out that the earth was formed out of the waters, that the waters were the first to receive the command to bring forth living creatures, and that our own human gestation takes place in water. *Stripping off old clothes, entering the waters naked, and then being clothed in a new white garment emphasized the complete rebirth of baptism.*

The next step in the baptism was the *final renunciation of Satan.*[4] While the renunciation of Satan was traditional in all the churches, a great deal of variety in the ceremony existed. In some churches the renunciation occurred as the candidate faced the west, the direction of Satan's kingdom. The candidate took off his other outer garment, stood on a piece of animal hide to symbolize the skins worn by Adam and Eve, and, with outstretched arms, renounced Satan. This action was followed by the allegiance to the triune

God in the words of the ancient creed, the forerunner of the Apostles' Creed, known as the interrogatory creed.[5] It asks for allegiance to the faith of the church, citing what the candidate believes about the Father, the Son, and the Holy Spirit. Faith is seen not merely as truth passed down from apostolic times but as a pact with Christ that replaces the pact with the devil.

After baptism, a symbol was developed to indicate *the seal of the Spirit*.[6] The seal of the Spirit expresses the conviction that all baptized believers have the indwelling Spirit, the seal of God's promise of salvation. According to Paul: "In him you also, when you have heard the word of truth, the gospel of your salvation, and had believed in him, were marked with the seal of the promised Holy Spirit" (Eph. 1:13).

Next, the newly baptized candidates, now members of the church, were brought into *full fellowship* with the Christian community. Now for the first time they were permitted to pray with the faithful and to give the kiss of peace. "And immediately thereafter they shall now pray with the faithful until all these are completed. And at the close of their prayer they shall give the kiss of peace."[7]

Finally, the converts were invited to participate for the first time in the *Eucharist*. Imagine how high the feelings must have run. The candidate had been in a long process of spiritual formation. On the Easter morning, after a long, perhaps arduous, yet meaningful journey into the waters of baptism, the convert was finally privileged to feast at the Table of the Lord.

Suggestions for Baptism in Your Church

The modern rites of baptism culminate the process of the journey to Christ and the church. From the very beginning, external rites have helped to form the internal reality of Christian conversion. Externally, these final services bring a person into the full fellowship of the church, and internally they enable the candidate to reenact the entire process of conversion. Baptism reenacts the death and resurrection of Christ as well as the convert's personal and subjective experience of being born anew.

Because baptism is celebrated in different ways among the churches today, it is difficult to prescribe how it may be done in your community. In the case of the Worship, Evangelism, and Nurture Mission, we are dealing with adults who have not been baptized. However, adults who have been baptized and are now returning to the church often do a reaffirmation of baptismal vows. Churches should follow their own traditions on these matters. Here are some suggestions:

Suggestions on How to Conduct the Rite of Baptism

- Prebaptismal preparation
  Encourage a time for fasting and prayer either on Friday and Saturday or on both days
- Establish an Easter eve paschal vigil service if possible. This service consists of four parts:[8]
  (1) the lighting of the fire
  (2) readings from the history of salvation
  (3) the baptism
  (4) the Easter Eucharist
- At the baptism or reaffirmation of baptism vows:
  (1) Ask the candidate, "Do you renounce the devil and all his works?" The candidate may answer with "Yes" and after a sign of rejection, such as "spitting" in the face of the devil.
  (2) Baptize the candidate according to your custom. For those who have been previously baptized, many churches will use a touch of water as a sign of their reaffirmation.

- The sign of receiving the Spirit
  After the baptism, sign the newly baptized with oil, saying, "Receive the Holy Spirit." Oil may be poured on the head and smeared on the face in a lavish style to express in a dramatic way the reception of the Spirit." For those who are reaffirming faith and have already received the sign of the Spirit, a drop of oil may be smeared on the forehead in the form of the cross, with a comment such as "let this oil remind you that you have been sealed with the Holy Spirit."
- The white robe
  After the sealing of the Spirit, cover the newly baptized and sealed person with a white robe or cloth around the shoulders to wear in the Easter Eucharist.
- Celebrate the Easter Eucharist.

Conclusion

I have shown that baptism was no ordinary rite in the early church and that it should be treated with enormous care and attention by our churches in the post-Christian setting.

In the process of the Worship, Evangelism, and Nurture Mission, baptism is a culminating act and a dramatic turning point. The convert has been working toward the baptismal moment for a long time. To treat the rite with carelessness or with a spirit of indifference is to disrespect and undermine the performative value of the rite. It is a moment that should never be forgotten, a moment that provides a visible tangible memory that can be unpacked as the memory of the meaning of spirituality. Baptismal spirituality is to always live in the pattern of Jesus' death and resurrection. A baptism with flare and drama fuels the memory of the baptized and continually ignites the drive to live the resurrected life.

Leader's Guide

A. EVALUATION
- How can you better inform your community of the breakdown of Christian values?
- What are you doing to inform your congregation, especially the young, of the difference between Christian spirituality and that of the New Age and Eastern spiritualities?
- Baptismal spirituality calls on us to turn away from evil and embrace the fruit of the Holy Spirit. How are you training your people (and the *kneeler*) to walk in the fruit of the Spirit?
- How do you fortify the faith of your people, and especially the *kneeler*, by the faith of the creed?
- How well are you doing in helping your people, and particularly the *kneeler*, in learning how to pray?
- How does this church handle spiritual warfare?

B. PLANNING A COURSE OF ACTION
   TO REVITALIZE THE CONGREGATION
- Call in a focus group made up of different members of the church to discuss the above questions. Listen to their answers.
- Read *Walk in the Spirit!* (Wheaton, Ill.: IWS Resources, 2001).

C. PLANNING A COURSE OF ACTION TO EQUIP THE KNEELER

- Examine *Walk in the Spirit!* (Wheaton, Ill.: IWS Resources, 2001).
- Will you use the one-on-one mentorship or a small group? Are these people adequately prepared to lead?
- How will you use or adapt the "scrutinies," or prayers, for the *kneelers* during worship?
- Discuss the details of your baptismal service.

Resources for Further Reading

A suggested resource for the *kneeler* is *Walk in the Spirit!* (Wheaton, Ill.: IWS Resources, 2001). Suggested resources for the leaders include James W. Fowler, *Becoming Adult, Becoming Christian* (San Francisco: Jossey-Bass Publishers, 2000), a helpful insight into the process of spiritual development; Ranald Macaulay and Jerram Barrs, *Being Human: The Nature of Spiritual Experience* (Downers Grove: InterVarsity Press, 1978), a work showing that spirituality is becoming more fully human; Eugene Peterson, *A Long Obedience in the Same Direction* (Downers Grove: InterVarsity Press, 1980), on the spirituality of endurance; Dallas Willard, *The Spirit of the Disciplines* (San Francisco: HarperSanFrancisco, 1991), a helpful guide to daily commitment; Alfred McBride and O. Praem, *The Ten Commandments: Covenant of Love* (Cincinnati: St. Anthony Messenger Press, 2001); Hans Urs Von Balthasar, *Prayer* (San Francisco: Ignatius, 1955); and William H. Willimon and Stanley Hauerwas, *Lord, Teach Us: The Lord's Prayer & The Christian Life* (Nashville: Abingdon Press, 1996).

V

Incorporating the Faithful

RECEIVING THE NEW MEMBER

JOURNEY TO JESUS

FAITHFUL

Spiritual Goal:
  Incorporation
Continuous Rite:
  Eucharist
Resource:
  Find Your Gift!

INTRODUCTION

Like everyone else, I have learned about my birth and infancy from my parents. They have described the little town in Pennsylvania where I was born, the aged family doctor, the rickety home hospital, the comments of the young nurse, and their own initial reactions to their newborn son. While I have no recollection of that event, I do know that I was loved, cared for, nursed, and coddled from the day I was born. That parental love and tender care saw me through my infancy and brought me into childhood. Without that parental aid and concern, I may not have grown to become a responsible member of the family.

Baptism needs to be seen like birth. Birth is not the beginning of life but a new phase. Even after a person has left the womb where he or she has been nurtured and cared for, the nurturing continues, but it is of a different kind. It's a socialization into a new community. My parents didn't put me in a parking lot and say, "If you're in need of anything, feel free to call on us." I needed to be incorporated into the family, to be fed, and nurtured from infancy to maturity. The same is true for the new Christian, who, after baptism, has now been birthed into the church and continues to need nurture and support. This is the purpose of the final phase—a period of continued nurture that fully incorporates the newly baptized into the life of the family, the local church.

13. Receiving New Members in the Ancient Church

Incorporation in the New Testament

The New Testament recognizes the new convert as an infant in the faith. For example, Peter refers to his reader as "newborn babes" and admonishes them to "long for the pure spiritual milk, that by it you may grow up to salvation" (1 Pet. 2:2 RSV). This concern for continued growth and nurture is captured by the writer of Hebrews, who urged his readers to "go on to maturity" (Heb. 6:1 RSV).

Likewise, Luke reports that when converts were brought into the body of Christ, "they devoted themselves to the apostles' teaching and fellowship, to the breaking of bread and the prayers" (Acts 2:42). Luke is describing instruction, worship, prayer, and fellowship—four of the major nutrients for a spiritually healthy infant.

The New Testament also gives us examples of converts who were nourished in the church. For example, Paul spent time with the disciples at Damascus after his conversion (Acts 9:20). While we don't know the subject of instruction, Paul's sermon in Acts 9:20 seems to suggest that the disciples spent some time nurturing Paul in the basic mysteries of the incarnation, death, and resurrection of Jesus. Timothy also received nourishment. Paul speaks of the nurture Timothy received from his grandmother and mother. "I am reminded of your sincere faith, a faith that lived first in your grandmother Lois and your mother Eunice and now, I am sure, lives in you" (2 Tim. 1:5). We also know of Paul's interest and concern for Timothy. Paul spoke of Timothy as "my beloved child" (2 Tim. 1:2). This endearing term certainly speaks of the personal nature of Paul's oversight and nurture of Timothy's spiritual life and subsequent ministry.

These examples demonstrate the heart of the incorporation period into the church: it is a time to integrate new converts into the household of faith. They are babes in Christ, infants who need to be reassured and received into the family of God's people, the church.

Incorporation in the Ancient Church

In the first three centuries, the newly baptized were integrated into a supportive community. Here they received personal support and direction. According to Hippolytus, new converts were expected to lead a life in keeping with their Christian commitment.[1] But the first order of spiritual business was to make them feel like members of the family. "We lead him to where those whom are called our brothers are assembled. We pray together fervently . . . then we give each other the kiss of peace."[2] Tertullian tells the candidates for baptism that after baptism they will "join hands with another and with their brother."[3] Clement of Alexandria, in a treatise entitled *To the Newly Baptized*, suggests that a new phase of spiritual development begins after baptism. The vision of Clement is that all of life is to be lived in the baptismal waters. Baptism must so permeate the Christian life that the baptized are not to depart from the image even in the thought patterns of sleep.[4]

The ancient church also developed symbols of incorporation. These symbols assisted the new converts in achieving a spiritual recollection of their baptism and stimulated them toward further growth. The most widespread postbaptismal symbol was the wearing of the white garment. The biblical origins of this lie in the Pauline metaphor of the new convert clothed in Christ (Gal. 3:27) and in John's assertion that the redeemed stand "before the throne and before the Lamb, robed in white" (Rev. 7:9).[5] White garments were worn for a full week after Easter, and the new members went to a daily service and heard sermons on the meaning of the Eucharist.

The newly baptized also wore white robes on Sundays during Easter season and sat together. The images of wearing white garments and of sitting together accented the importance of this period and made the entire congregation conscious of the new members' integration into the church. It also imaged the evangelistic mission of the church. Some scholars connect the wearing of the white robe with the picture of worship in the heavens:

> After this I looked, and there was a great multitude that no one could count, from every nation, from all tribes and peoples and languages, standing before the throne and before the Lamb, robed in white. . . . Then one of the elders addressed me, saying, "Who are these, robed in white, and where have they come from?" . . . Then he said . . . "These are they who . . . have washed their robes and made them white in the blood of the Lamb." (Rev. 7:9, 13-14)

This is a beautiful and moving image for the newly baptized. Baptism into Christ and the church was no casual thing. By becoming baptized, a person was expressing his or her willingness to die for Christ—a powerful statement, especially in the middle of the third century when Decius had initiated a systematic persecution to rid the Roman Empire of Christians. The persecution didn't halt the growth of the church. So many new converts poured into the church that Tertullian was moved to say that the blood of martyrs is the seed of the church.

Postbaptismal Instruction

The instruction given to the newly baptized during the postbaptismal period continued to lead them on the path of spiritual growth. During this time they were known as the *faithful*.

Considerable attention was given to *spiritual instruction*. For example, John Chrysostom stressed the ongoing battle with the powers of Satan and the need to be vigilant against the powers of evil. He instructed the *faithful* that though "you have indeed been baptized . . . if you are not led by the Spirit of God, you will have lost the dignity which has been conferred upon you."[6] The emphasis, like that of the Paul's letter to the Hebrews was to "hold fast to the confession of our hope" (Heb. 10:23) and to persevere "so that when you have done the will of God, you may receive what was promised" (Heb. 10:36).

The postbaptismal period was also a time to deal with the incorporation of the faithful into the church. The new convert had been participating in the life of the church since the rite of conversion. However, baptism brought the convert into a new relationship. Now the converting person was a full member of the church. It was then time to discern his or her gifts and to give the new member a ministry in the church. The spiritual mentor may have been especially helpful in this task.

Third, the postbaptismal period heightens the new convert's *concern for the world*. This concern refers to Christ's giving himself for the salvation of the world. The church at worship and work is the sign of this redemption. Consequently, the church cannot be an entity unto itself in the world. What the soul is to the body, the church is to the world. The church not only prays for the world, but also acts on behalf of it. It opposes, by words and actions, the evil powers that rage. Nurturing time involves new converts in action as well as in prayer for the needs of the world. Concern for the poor and needy, the oppressed, the elderly, the uneducated, the rights of the unborn, the environment, and so on, can be acted on by the new Christian.

Finally, postbaptismal instruction included a time for the *faithful* to "understand the *paschal mystery* more fully and to bring it into their lives."[7] During the conversion journey, the convert has only heard of the eucharistic celebration or seen it from afar. Now, having been baptized, the *faithful* enjoys the spiritually refreshing privilege of celebrating at the Lord's Table on a regular basis. According to Egira, an eyewitness to the period of the faithful in Jerusalem in the fourth century, the mysteries were unveiled so well that "no one can remain unmoved by what they hear."[8]

The experience of tasting the death and resurrection of Jesus at the Table of the Lord is a new stage in the *faithful's* spiritual journey. It is a spiritual privilege gained, a new source of spiritual sustenance. In the symbolic presentation of the death and resurrection of Christ, the heart of the Christian gospel is proclaimed. Consequently, the earnest believer will experience a continual renewal of his or her relationship with God through Christ at the Table of the Lord. In addition, when that relationship is broken or in need of repair, the *faithful* may experience an inner spiritual healing at the Eucharist.

If one applies the axiom "You cannot understand what you have not experienced" to the nurturing period, it becomes apparent that the experience of God's saving and sustaining presence at the Table of the Lord needs to be explored with the *faithful*. Because bread and wine are ultimately mysteries of God's saving action, there is no way to define or intellectually exhaust the mystery. Rather, postbaptismal time allows the *faithful* to share his or her experience at the Table of the Lord and to grow in a deeper experience of God's loving grace.

Postbaptismal time is the follow-up. It solidifies conversion *within* the church, emphasizing that life in Christ is not a lonesome journey, but one in the context of community. Its biblical roots are captured in the image of the spiritual infant. Its historical image is best pictured by the white-robed throng gathered at the daily Eucharist. These new

Christians are integrated into the inner life of the church so that they may learn full participation in the body of Christ, commit themselves to a caring and responsible relationship to the world, and find continual spiritual nourishment at God's table.

14. Receiving New Members Today

We have now come to the fourth phase of the *Journey to Jesus*. During this period, the congregation needs to pay attention to four matters:

- making the new members feel welcome
- discerning their gifts
- impressing upon them their call to be stewards of creation
- empowering them to be witnesses

Make New Members Feel Welcome

Scholars of New Testament Christianity point out that "the primary way in which the church in Jerusalem grew was through fellowship."[1] Because the church is about a new humanity, fellowship and relationship in community is a key for continued personal spiritual growth and for staying the course. The writer of Hebrews suggests this idea in the context of expressing the need for perseverance in the faith: "Let us not give up meeting together, as some are in the habit of doing, but let us encourage one another" (Heb. 10:25 NIV). In church and in worship we support and encourage one another, for here we are "fellow citizens with God's people and members of God's household" (Eph. 2:19 NIV).

When a baby is born, the parents shower the child with attention. In the same manner there is a need for the church to pay special attention to the newly baptized. Have new members wear white robes and sit together during the Sundays of Easter, or develop some other appropriate traditions. Take time to think through how you may provide images and memories for the newly baptized. Remember "hospitality is a way of life fundamental to Christian identity."[2]

Discern Gifts

Make the second concern of the faithful period a time to discern and use gifts. To accomplish this goal, most churches will have to change from the model of congregational dependence to the model of interdependence.

Greg Ogden refers to ministry in the traditional Protestant church as the "dependency model." He writes that it "views pastors as the performers who enact 'real' ministry, while God's people are the audience who passively write reviews of the actors' efforts."[3] The problematic view stems from the institutionalization of the church—a model followed by most Protestant churches. Instead, the "organism" model of the church[4] must be recovered. The starting point is our view of leadership. The Protestant view of leadership can be traced back to the Reformation and the doctrines of both Luther and Calvin who taught that the church is found "wherever the Word is rightly preached and the sacraments are rightly administered." The focus lies on the pastor and what the pastor is *doing* for the people. The starting point for an organism view of leadership is the body of Christ from which the gifts arise. This view is rooted in the biblical notion of "assembly." It claims the primary focus of God's Spirit is found in the assembly and in the giftedness of the people. The organism model puts the focus on the presence of God within the community and stresses each person's calling to be Jesus to one another.

The typical Protestant top-down approach to ministry squelches the gifts of the people and the "everybody is a minister" theology of the priesthood of all believers. This current "dependency model" is a distortion of the Reformers' intention. The Reformers recognized the priestly ministry of all of God's people, but placed the particular ministry of preaching and the celebration of the sacrament in a specific ordained office. In time, the pastoral office became "separated out" from the office of gifts given to all the people. This tragic development resulted in two peoples and two levels within the church: the clergy and the laity. The language of ministry (meaning the one who holds divine office) and layperson (meaning the one who does not hold an office) furthered the notion that "laypeople" are "acted upon" by the "actor." Consequently, congregations became passive supporters of the minister, who became the professional Christian among them. Today's new language calls all of God's people "ministers." Within the ministry of all, there are some who have the ministry of pastor. This language breaks down the false distinction between "minister" and "lay," and at least linguistically returns the call of ministry to all of God's people in the body of Christ.

To illustrate how all of God's people are ministers, Ogden retells an apocryphal story taken from Elizabeth O'Conner: "Michelangelo was pushing a large chunk of stone down the street toward his sculpting studio when a neighbor cried out, 'Hey, Michael, what are you going to do with that old piece of stone?' Michelangelo replied, 'There is an angel in there that wants to come out.'"[5]

The work of the pastor and all the ministers of the church during the period of the faithful is to chisel the stone of the new believer and let the gift emerge. In Ephesians 4:11-16, Paul argues for the "everyone is a minister" perspective:

> The gifts he gave were that some would be apostles, some prophets, some evangelists, some pastors and teachers, to equip the saints for the work of ministry, for building up the body of Christ . . . to maturity, to the measure of the full stature of Christ. We must no longer be childrem . . . we must grow up in every way into him who is the head . . . from whom the whole body, joined

175

and knit together by every ligament with which it is equipped, . . . promotes the body's growth in building itself up in love.

Elton Trueblood rightly states, "The pastorate is for those who possess the peculiar gift of being able to help other men and women to practice any ministry to which they are called."[6] But how are we to implement this model? The model presented today is that of the superstar pastor. For example, R. Paul Stevens, in *Liberating the Laity*, tells how he once asked a group of seminary students whether they were being taught the model in which the pastor is the key equipper of the congregation. They answered, "That's what we're taught, but the model pastors brought in to the seminary for us to meet are usually the superstars."[7]

We need to humble ourselves and turn away from "minister stardom." The calling of the pastor is to help new members discover the gift given to them by God for the mutual ministry of all God's people. Following Paul, we need to remember that "we have gifts that differ according to the grace given to us" (Rom. 12:6*a*).

> If a man's gift is prophesying, let him use it in proportion to his faith. If it is serving, let him serve; if it is teaching, let him teach; if it is encouraging, let him encourage; if it is contributing to the needs of others, let him give generously; if it is leadership, let him govern diligently; if it is showing mercy, let him do it cheerfully. (Rom. 12:6-8 NIV)

But how are we to find and release the gifts of the people? Melvin Steinbron suggests nine ways. These "marks," as he calls them, may help you to incorporate everyone into the full life of the church and encourage each to find and use his or her special ministry gift within the body: Here are the steps:

- An intentional, well-defined strategy.
- A *programmatic provision to enable people to discover their gifts, to hear God's call, and to come forward to commit themselves to a ministry.
- Publicizing specific equipping opportunities and schedules.
- A process for presenting a "menu" of ministries from which people can choose. This process replaces using delegation, appointment, or election to determine where individuals should serve—"filling slots" as someone called it.
- An every-member ministry preaching and teaching priority, thereby making the biblical teachings on spiritual gifts and divine call well known by the new members.
- Communicating the high-level expectation to new members that every member of the church will be serving God in some specific ministry.
- Lay** readers model their every-member ministry orientation.
- Clergy and other staff leaders relinquish ministry to gifted and equipped laypeople.
- People are comfortable with the goal of every-member ministry—the expectations, procedures, theology, and terminology—as characteristics of the culture of their church.[8]

* I suggest dropping the word programmatic; the author probably means "a process by which people are enabled."
** Drop the word "lay."

We have seen that an essential aspect of spiritual integration into the community is in helping the *faithful* discover the gift God has given them in ministry. Whatever their gift—the ministry of hospitality, greeting, music, ushering, caring for the property, or one of many other gifts—find it and release it.

The Call to Be Stewards of Creation

A third area of attention during the new member period is to make certain that each person knows how all of his or her work and life is under the calling of God.

Theologian Paul Lakeland writes: "Theologies of redemption . . . offered only to the human race and not . . . integral to the entire universe . . . are inadequate."[9] In the postmodern world, Christians need to pay special attention to the environment, to the world, and even to the cosmos. This perspective is rooted in the biblical and classical view of salvation. It speaks against the reduction of salvation to human creatures only, and affirms that God's work of salvation is directed toward the whole cosmos. I can remember when Christians used language such as "let's witness to souls" or "thirty souls came to know Jesus." This language was challenged in the 1950s and beyond as people came to embrace a more holistic sense of the person. It was recognized that "soul" language was a Gnostic rejection of the flesh. This language made it appear that the only thing God cared about was a disembodied soul somehow imprisoned in a human body. While body and soul are now commonly linked together in a psychosomatic unity, there still remains a human creature/creation dichotomy in much Christian thinking. Lakeland is right, that this kind of speech will not communicate adequately in a postmodern ecologically sensitive world.

The call to be concerned about the world is first rooted in the creation narratives. The text of Genesis 1 says: "God blessed them, and God said to them, 'Be fruitful and multiply; and fill the earth and subdue it; and have dominion over the fish of the sea and over the birds of the air and over every living thing that moves upon the earth' " (v. 28). And the text of Genesis 2 says: "The Lord God took the man and put him in the garden of Eden to till it and keep it" (v. 15). These imperatives have been called the "cultural mandate." Christians have recognized that the vocation of developing civilization, of being caretakers of the earth, of being coworkers with God in creation are all rooted in these accounts.

The fall of Adam and Eve clearly represents the damaging effects of sin on the created order. In a classic passage on the cosmic impact of sin, Paul refers to "the creation . . . subjected to frustration" and in "bondage to decay" (Rom. 8:20, 21 NIV). The work of Christ, according to this passage, and to the whole narrative of biblical history is to "liberate" the creation from its "bondage" and to bring it into "the glorious freedom of the children of God" (Rom. 8:21). Paul is so confident of the salvation of the entire cosmos in the eschatological coming of Christ that he sees the world pregnant with its own restoration accomplished by the work of Christ: "We know that the whole creation has been groaning as in the pains of childbirth right up to the present time" (Rom. 8:22). This salvation of the whole creation is rooted in the incarnation, death, resurrection, and second coming of Christ. God did not just step into history to save souls or to save persons alone, but to rescue the entire creation. Through Jesus, the second Adam, he reversed the sin of the first Adam, and by his death conquered the power of death, which still exercises its power in the world today. But at his coming, all powers will be put out of service forever, creation will be released from its bondage, and death will be no more.

The new member is taught to think and pray from this perspective. This is the time to inform the new Christian that the role of the church in the world is to be a "living witness" to this reality. Each member of the church should see his or her calling in life to live and work in the world in such a way that the real truth about the world is made evident.

For this reason each of us, as members of the church, are called to be "priests of creation."[10] We act as stewards of God's earth in our work and leisure, lovingly caring for the ecological system in anticipation of its freedom from the powers of evil that operate through the various structures. In worship we celebrate the reversal of the Fall, and in our work we celebrate our calling to work redemptively in the world. We bring order out of chaos, and strive to repair the broken world. As priests of creation, we are not self-centered, but adapt the attitude of repairing, renewing, and restoring all of life. We care for the poor; we right wrongs; we stand for justice; we support the sanctity of life; we affirm integrity in work, play, leisure; we offer our lives to God; we are ethical and moral. And in all of this, we serve God's purposes in the world. For the work and service we do toward God, "offered by humanity in gratitude for what God has done to save and renew creation[,] always has worth in God's eyes."[11]

Be My Witness

It is interesting that as soon as the disciples on the road to Emmaus realized that it was the resurrected Jesus who broke bread with them, they immediately ran back to Jerusalem to tell the other disciples. The end of the spiritual formation journey for the seeker is a new beginning. Now that the new member has been nurtured into faith, he or she can become one who nurtures. It is hoped that the new members have been "talking up" the faith through the entire journey. Now they in turn can mentor others into the faith!

In sum, during their time of incorporation into the church, the new members learn several strategic realities of the Christian life. First, the gifts given to them by God are to be used to serve God's work within the church. And second, gifts of vocation and calling in life are used in the service of God as well. In this, the new members discover there is no bifurcation between the secular and the sacred. For the Christian, all things are sacred because God created and became incarnated in Jesus to restore, recover, and renew creation to be completed at the end of history. Worship and work point to Christian stewardship in the redeemed world for all who know how to see. Having seen Jesus and tasted of new life, the new member is ready to tell others and mentor them into faith.

15. The Rite of Eucharist

The final rite of *Journey to Jesus*, one that is continually repeated, is that of eating the bread and drinking the wine within and among the community. Baptism was the rite of entry, the Table is the rite of fellowship with God and each other. We are only baptized once, but we eat forever. Because eating is such a powerful symbol, we turn to examine what eating at God's table means and what it does.

What Eating at God's Table Means

Perhaps the most profound act in which we engage in the church is eating and drinking together. Eating at God's table brings into sharp focus everything experienced during the entire journey to Christ and into the church, for it signifies the faith of the church.

First, table worship verbally and symbolically expresses the *Missio Dei* of the triune God, especially in the prayer that is said over the bread and wine. This is illustrated by the prayer of thanksgiving written down as a guideline by Hippolytus in *The Apostolic Tradition*:

> We render thanks to you, O God, through your beloved child Jesus Christ, whom in the last times you sent to us as saviour and redeemer and angel of your will; who is your inseparable Word, through whom you made all things, and in whom you were well pleased.
>
> You sent him from heaven into the Virgin's womb; and, conceived in the womb, he was made flesh and was manifested as your Son, being born of the Holy Spirit and the Virgin.
>
> Fulfilling your will and gaining for you a holy people,

he stretched out his hands when he should suffer, that he might release from suffering those who have believed in you.

And when he was betrayed to voluntary suffering that he might destroy death, and break the bonds of the devil, and tread down hell, and shine upon the righteous, and fix the limit, and manifest the resurrection, he took bread and gave thanks to you, saying, "Take, eat; this is my body, which shall be broken for you." Likewise also the cup, saying, "This is my blood, which is shed for you; when you do this, you make my remembrance."

Remembering therefore his death and resurrection, we offer to you the bread and the cup, giving you thanks because you have held us worthy to stand before you and minister to you.

And we ask that you would send your Holy Spirit upon the offering of your holy Church; that, gathering them into one, you would grant to all who partake of the holy things (to partake) for the fullness of the Holy Spirit for the confirmation of faith in truth; that we may praise and glorify you through your child Jesus Christ, through whom be glory and honour to you, to the Father and the Son with the Holy Spirit, in your holy Church, both now and to the ages of ages. (Amen.)[1]

In this ancient prayer, the Father sends the Son, who is victorious over the powers of evil. The Holy Spirit is sent to unite the church, to fill and empower the Christian and to confirm faith in truth.

This prayer expresses all four marks of the missional church. First, the prayer is a profound proclamation and enactment of *Christus Victor:*

"When He was betrayed to voluntary suffering that he might *abolish death* and *rend (break) the bonds of death*, and *enlighten the righteous* (a term frequently used in ancient worship is 'open the way to heaven'; another term that is frequently used is 'restore the nature of man') and establish the limit (this refers to the limitations imposed upon the powers) and demonstrate the resurrection (a second act of creation, a beginning again which now occurs in the church)."

Second, the prayer of thanksgiving points to the *mothering role of the church*, for it recalls the family narrative, the story that actualizes, brings into being, and concretizes the experience of being the people of God. Third, it is a *performative symbol* in that it not only speaks the story but also *performs* the story in the drama of the breaking of the bread and the lifting of the cup. Finally, the process of coming before God, hearing the story of salvation, and ingesting bread and wine makes the Eucharist a culminating event. It is an event of remembrance, of the moment, and one that foreshadows the kingdom reality of God's peace that will rest over the entire created order.

In many churches today, the meaning, profundity, power, and joy of Eucharist worship have been lost. Because of the modern scientific way of seeing things, we have lost the connection between the food as known and the food as experienced. Science is only interested in fact, not meaning.[2] Science says, "This is food." Meaning says, "This is relationship with the triune God whom we praise, the Son whom we remember, the Spirit whom we experience." So bread and wine are seen primarily as the result of the science of agriculture and bread making, and not viewed in the spiritual sense of the provision made by the Creator to sustain the creatures whom God loves. In science, nature is viewed as the phenomena of chance, the result of evolution, the material condition of life. But as Christians, we are to see much deeper. In eating and drinking, we celebrate a personal loving Creator who is the Meaning-giver of life.

The very narrative of life that we recall, tell, and celebrate in worship, culminating at the Eucharist, is replete with references to eating. The Bible and the Christian story are food-driven. We lost our relationship to God in the Garden over a rebellious act of eating. But God comes to us again and again and, through the sign of eating, restores the relationship. The theophany of God with Abraham was in the context of food (Genesis 18); the exodus from Egypt was accompanied by the sign of eating (Exodus 12); instructions regarding the Passover included eating as remembrance of God's provision (Numbers 9); the promise of God's continued presence with Israel was manna (Numbers 11); the reaffirmation of the covenant with God after Israel returned from exile was a joyous feast (Neh. 8:10); the Gospel accounts frequently reference Jesus eating with his disciples, with crowds, or with sinners (Mark 6, 8); Jesus describes his relation to his disciples with the analogy of food (John 6); before his death, he ate with his disciples (Luke 22); after his resurrection, he appeared to the disciples in the breaking of bread (Luke 24); the primitive Christian community ate together (Acts 2); Jesus commanded us to eat as a way of *anamnesis*, a remembrance that continually makes him present in eating; and the celebration of God's final victory over the powers of evil will be the great messianic banquet (Rev. 19:9).

Eating at the table means and signifies a relationship with God. We recognize the analogy of relationship in our human eating. We generally choose to eat with people we *want* to eat with. Eating is the context in which relationships are established and maintained, sometimes repaired, and we hope deepened and even transformed. It not only means relationship, it *does* relationship.

What Eating at God's Table Does

If eating means relationship, we must ask, "What is the process by which eating forms relationship?"

First, consider how eating is a transfer of life. What we eat is life-giving because it gave its life for us. This is particularly true when we eat natural or unprocessed food. When we eat meat, vegetables, grain, or fruit, we eat what has or had a real life from a womb, from the ground, from a bush, from the seed. But it had life to give us because it received life from a previous form of life that gave its life in eating.

Human beings are the only members of God's creatures in this world who do not give their life as material food to another creature. Humans are at the top of the food chain. But not so spiritually. God sent God's only Son, the Word, united with the man Jesus, to be our spiritual food. By his life-giving death, Jesus poured out the life of his body, his blood, so that his blood and body does for us what we cannot do for ourselves—Jesus does relationship for us with God. In this way, God, who is the creator and life-giver of all material food is also the life-giver of our spiritual living. God gave us life in creation and we rebelled against it. God sent Jesus to give it to us again, but this time God gave up life through God's Son so that we may have what the early church called his "life-giving cross." By ingesting bread and wine, we take into ourselves the life-giving sacrifice of Jesus through whom death is conquered. Bread and wine, eaten and drunk in faith, is the reality of receiving God's life within, through which we are spiritually and physically nourished and sustained. Bread and wine is creation becoming incarnation so that we may become re-creation.

Second, eating at the Table is never done alone, but in community with others of the faith, creating social formation. Eating is most enjoyable when done *together*. Eating alone lacks the power of formation with another, cannot be a shared experience, and may feed the body but rarely feeds the soul. Christianity is not individualistic, and eating at God's table is not designed to be done in isolation. Like all good meals, it not only expresses community but also creates it. Good table worship is therefore remembered with fondness and looked forward to with eager anticipation, for it brings us out of ourselves and gives us the opportunity to experience our communal nature formed in the image of God's triune nature.

Finally, eating together, because it is a transfer of God's life to us and an experience of the social community of God's life, is a transforming experience. Good food is metabolized into good nutrients in our body, giving us health, strength, and vitality. Poor food does the opposite; it breaks down in ways that have a negative effect on our health. "You are what you eat," the saying goes. Eat poor quality food, suffer bad health. Eat good quality food, experience vibrant health. The transforming power of bread and wine is an experience of ingesting the second Adam. He is the only one who reverses the damage of the "bad apple," to use a metaphor. The bread and the wine are symbols of God's provision for the spiritual and physical transformation of our lives and of the whole cosmos. The edible objects are thoroughly transformed by and re-formed into the eater. That is why it may be necessary for some congregations to rethink the way they eat and drink together.

Rethinking the Way We Eat at God's Table

Most of us can remember an experience of eating at someone's home where the host was courteous but not warm; where communication was stilted, hesitant, perhaps even forced; where the surrounding environment lacked luster, perhaps even dulling to the senses. On the other hand, we are probably quite capable of remembering occasions just the opposite. The host was warm and inviting, leaving us with the sense that the host wanted us to be there; communication was free, open, and engaging; the environment was bright, colorful, and full of cheer. Compare these instances. The analogy is clear. One experience was sober and joyless—the kind we don't want to repeat. The other was full of meaning and joy, the kind we want to repeat.

In many churches, the experience of eating at God's table is sober, uninviting, tense, and boring. The *faithful*, in their first Eucharist and in all succeeding experiences of eating at God's table, need a refreshing and joyous experience of the meaning of eating. The content of the food—how it is presented, prayed for, and received—is of utmost importance. There is a need to recapture the warmth of God, the joy of eating, the transfer of God's power to our lives, the formation of community. For it is here in this act of eating that the *faithful* will find their continual refreshment and sustenance in the food that, by the power of the Holy Spirit, confirms faith in truth.

In this section we have been concerned with the final stage of the *Journey to Jesus*. How do you successfully incorporate the seeker, who has traveled through various phases of faith, into the full life of the church? The rite of Eucharist completes the process. But, as with any good final stage, it simply represents a new beginning. Now the seeker is a member of the faithful, a living witness to the reality of God. By letting new converts find their place in the body; by giving them continual sustenance in the Eucharist; by offering personal spiritual guidance in the Word, dependence on God in prayer, and a sense of belonging in the community, the new Christian will continue on the road.

Leader's Guide

A. EVALUATE THE EFFECTIVENESS OF YOUR CONGREGATION IN THESE AREAS:

- How can you improve your hospitality to guests and new members?
- Have you adequately identified and unleashed the gifts of all your people?
- Does this community have a sense of God's calling in every area of life and work, or do you function out of a secular/sacred dichotomy?
- How could you improve your empowerment of each person's call to be a witness to family, friends, neighbors, and fellow workers?
- Do your people have an experience of the mystery and power of the Eucharist?

B. PLANNING A COURSE OF ACTION TO REVITALIZE THE CONGREGATION

- Call together a focus group and ask them to reflect on the questions above. Then call for suggestions that will help to order and organize the congregation into a more effective incorporation.

C. PLANNING A COURSE OF ACTION TO EQUIP THE KNEELER

- Review *Find Your Gift!* (Wheaton, Ill.: IWS Resources, 2001).
- Assign persons for a one-on-one mentorship.
- Teach the *Find Your Gift!* study.
- Identify the *faithfuls'* gifts and incorporate them into the life of the church.

Resources for Further Reading

A suggested resource for the *faithful* is *Find Your Gift!* (Wheaton, Ill.: IWS Resources, 2001), this booklet instructs Christians on the life of the church, helps them discern the gift they bring, and encourages them to do servanthood ministry in the church and in the world. Suggested resources for the congregation are Greg Ogden, *The New Reformation: Returning the Ministry to the People of God* (Grand Rapids: Zondervan, 1980); and Don and Katie Fortune, *Discover Your God-given Gifts* (Grand Rapids: Baker Books, 1987).

Other suggested resources for the congregation: to identify hospitality, read Christine Pohl, *Making Room: Recovering Hospitality in the Christian Tradition* (Grand Rapids: Eerdmans, 1999); to return ministry to the people, read Greg Ogden, *The New Reformation: Returning Ministry to the People of God* (Grand Rapids: Zondervan, 1990); Melvin J. Steinbron, *The Lay-Driven Church: How to Empower the People in Your Church to Share the Tasks of Ministry* (Ventura, Calif.: Regal, 1997); and Henry A. Simon, *Mentoring* (St. Louis: Concordia Publishing House, 2001).

16. Implementing *Journey to Jesus*

I have been lecturing on the Worship, Evangelism, and Nurture Mission of the third-century church to my class for years. One of my students, Louis, took up the challenge to apply this process to the local church he pastors in Illinois. In a recent visit with him, he made some interesting observations.

"I'm attracted to this approach to church growth," Louis said, "because it doesn't put sociological studies in the driver's wheel and relegate theology to the backseat. Instead, this historic approach to bringing people into the faith calls for a strenuous and demanding discipleship. It doesn't just baptize the culture or put a Christian veneer on the American dream. It's characterized by substance; it has teeth to it. I constantly urge my congregation to make a distinction between superficial Christianity and the real thing, and this process makes what I preach happen."

Louis introduced his version of the historic model of Worship, Evangelism, and Nurture to his congregation with four convictions. First, good worship is the key. Worship has to be biblical and God-centered. Worship does not focus on "me and my experience" but on "God and God's work in history for me and the whole creation." Second, the process has to be theological. The church must avoid the latest gimmick or trend, and develop a model of new life that is rooted in the biblical concept of growth. Good journeys of spiritual formation are characterized by affirming Christian lifestyle values and embracing practices of prayer, Scripture reading, witness, and helping the needy. Third, a discipleship process must be relationally connected. It cannot reflect an isolated individualistic

Christianity, but one that is worked out in the context of true community. Fourth, new Christians are to come into the church as contributors. They need to embrace their new identity as believers, accept their own unique giftedness and offer themselves in service to the church. In this way, Louis says, "Spiritual formation becomes an ascendant aspect of our lives. We grow and continue to grow in the faith as we pass through the stages into a deeper relationship with Jesus."

"Fundamentally," says Louis, "I see myself as a spiritual tour guide. As I lead my people through the process of spiritual formation and carry them through the various stages of passage rites, they are drawn into the essence of the faith through ritual patterns. Questions such as who we are and what we are called to be are continually set forth, in this way the church is allowed to become the church and the people are repeatedly called into the seriousness of what it means to be committed Christians. Through this process, my people connect with a stream of people that go back two thousand years. They know they stand in their wake and share in their faith. Like their predecessors, they continually ask what does it mean to be a faithful disciple? I want my people to avoid being drawn into current cultural values. So I always strive to create a certain level of discomfort with their present state of spirituality so that they continue to grow. I always keep in mind Luther's mandate that each person must do his or her own believing even as they must do their own dying. This process keeps us on our spiritual toes."

"However, my experience," Louis cautions, "is that about 10 percent of the congregation will become truly committed to the process. That 10 percent makes my work highly rewarding. . . . The results are worth the effort."

Keep Louis's advice in mind as you introduce the *Journey to Jesus* to your congregation in a way that is *indigenous to them.* The *Journey* is characterized by an elasticity that allows it to bend and be shaped by each congregation.

In this final chapter, I will present the more fixed elements of the *Journey to Jesus*. Here is the place to start. Then, as you move into the experience of the *Journey*, take the liberties with it that come naturally and reflect the experience of your congregation: Learning how to do the *Journey to Jesus* is like learning anything else. You at first follow the rules closely until you understand how it works. Then you introduce your own style to the process and imprint it with your particular character.

In the introduction, I asked you to read this book with the following question in mind: "What will it take for my congregation to do this kind of evangelism?" Here, then, are the five major questions you need to address as you establish the *Journey to Jesus* in your church.

1. What kind of congregation does it take?
2. What ministries are needed?
3. What is the time factor?
4. What type of structure is needed?
5. How do we get started?

What Kind of Congregation Does It Take?

The *Journey to Jesus* can be done by any congregation that is committed to being a missional church in this post-Christian world. This kind of congregation has the following characteristics:

First, it preaches that God's mission in Jesus Christ is to transform lives and to redeem creation. This message needs to be clearly understood and proclaimed to all members and seekers.

Second, it is animated by this good news. That is, the life-giving message of the gospel needs to be internalized by the congregation and find expression in the spirit of the people. It should be expressed in the energy of the people in hospitality, worship, education, spiritual formation, social service, and all the ministries of the church.

Third, the worship, evangelism and nurture congregation needs to be open to growth and inclusion of new members. The people need to share with others the gospel and new life they have found. They should intentionally reach out to bring others into the church, because they love their community and find that the warmth, love and excitement of being together is fulfilling and strengthens them in faith. This kind of congregation is contagious and energetic. When you are among them you are apt to say, "Something's going on here and I want to be part of this group."

Fourth, a worship, evangelism and nurture congregation listens to the text of culture. These people know what's going on in the world and care about it. They create ministry groups to offer help, counsel and direction for people affected by the diseases and decay of society. These people are authentic: they are not given to false and prideful images of the self. They share their own brokenness and failures and accept people where they are. They want an intergenerational and multicultural community. They live out what it means to be the presence of Jesus Christ in the world, a community that looks like and really is an alternative culture of people shaped by the vision of the kingdom of God.

These four conditions are essential features of the Worship, Evangelism, and Nurture Mission. They call the congregation to a serious Christian discipleship and represent the *ideal* toward which the church strives. Remember, Louis found a core of 10 percent of the people committed to the mission, and for him that was enough to get started, and adequate encouragement to keep going. If 10 percent of your congregation have a high level of commitment, let

them do *Journey to Jesus* as a trial run. It will ignite enthusiasm and generate greater involvement the second time
around. If 10 percent of your congregation, or even less, will
journey through the four stages reading; studying, and
sharing the four supplemental books *(Follow Me!, Be My
Disciple!, Walk in the Spirit!, Find Your Gift!)* and go through
the passage rites, their lives will be transformed. They then
will become the core group of people who lead the congregation the next year in a more effective experience of the
Worship, Evangelism, and Nurture Mission of the church.

What Ministries Are Needed?

In order for a congregation to do the Journey to Jesus,
several ministries must emerge. First, someone needs to
oversee the entire process, be in charge. This person may be
called the *pastor of spiritual formation.* His or her responsi-
bilities include the following:

(1) An understanding of the entire mission. This person
may begin to understand the mission by carefully reading
this book and by studying the chart on page 207 until they
are able to recite from memory the main feature of each of
the four stages, the basic idea of each of the supplemental
books, and the purpose and basic content of the passage
rites. At first glance, all of this material may seem overwhelming. However, as it is read, studied, digested, and
especially *done,* it will become as familiar as one's native
language. Like anything else, something worth doing takes
time and experimentation. Expect to make mistakes, to get
confused, and to feel overwhelmed. It's all part of the
process. But be persistent, for in the end the "payoff" is
well worth the struggle.

(2) An ability to work with people and know how to
direct people in a noncontrolling way. A controlling person
or person who seeks to micromanage the entire process
will thwart the process and prevent the freedom to work
creatively and personally in the process.

(3) Thoroughly acquainted with the suggestions made in the *Leader's Guide* that appears at the end of each section. There is no need to follow these directions in a slavish manner. The leader of each congregation should feel free to adapt this material so that it fits the ethos of the local church.

Second, a *worship leader* needs to be appointed to oversee the passage rites that convey the converting persons' transition from one stage of the *Journey to Jesus* to the next. This ministry includes the following:

(1) The worship leader needs to become intensely conversant with the voice of each passage rite. What is this passage rite doing? How does it function as a bridge from one stage of conversion to the next?

(2) Once the worship leader is conversant with the nature, the content and the purpose of the passage rites, the leader must then translate this rite into a language that captures the voice of his or her congregation. The rites included in this book are meant to be adapted. For a liturgical church, the rites may be made more liturgical, for a free church, they need to be translated in such a way that they express the common language of the people.

(3) The worship leader needs to prepare a worship setting for the rites. What kind of music is needed to accompany the rites? What kind of atmosphere? How will this be choreographed? All these questions are to be handled by the worship leader in cooperation with the pastor of spiritual formation, who offers the general oversight over the entire process.

The third set of persons intrinsically involved in making the *Journey to Jesus* happen are the *personal mentors and the small-group leaders*. The personal mentor gives the converting person one-on-one guidance, and the group leader offers leadership and spiritual guidance to two or more persons who meet in a small group setting on a regular basis. The guidance offered by the personal mentor or small-group leader will revolve around the study and discussion of the *Journey to Jesus* booklets. Each booklet serves a particular stage of the journey. Each booklet is based on Scripture studies and calls upon both the mentor or small-group leader as well as the converting persons to hear the voice of God in Scripture.

As the converting and growing person is exposed to what it means to be a Christian, what is a disciple, why does one need to be equipped by the Holy Spirit to live the Christian life, and how does one find and use his or her gift, that person is not brought to the "end" of the journey but more to the "beginning." The whole process is an initiation into the faith, an initiation that sets forth a trajectory for lifelong growth.

The Pastor of Spiritual Formation Supervises the Process

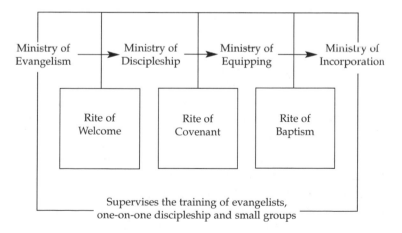

Mentors and small-group leaders need to see their own role as that of a "fellow traveler." If mentors or leaders approach their ministry with the attitude of "I've got it, and you don't have it, but when you go through the passage rite you'll have it too," the wrong signal will be sent. The mentor and small-group leader need to approach the ministry with the converting person with the attitude that "we are on this journey together, we are both learning and growing deeper, there is no end to how much God may give us from Scripture, so let's look at this together because we are both growing."

The work of the one person who is the minister and servant of all the personal mentors and the small-group leaders is more than that of organizing, but it is to journey together toward a deeper experience of Jesus. The pastor of spiritual formation walks the journey as well and leads the personal mentors and small-group leaders so that they in turn can provide the right kind of mentoring and leadership to the converting persons.

What Is the Time Factor for the *Journey to Jesus?*

The time factor for the *Journey to Jesus* is certainly flexible. The seeker stage is obviously indeterminate. A person may be converted to Christ quickly, or it may take months or even years. The booklet *Follow Me!* which is designed to lead a person to think about his or her spiritual condition and the transforming power of Christ, contains ten meditations. When a person meditates on these in sequence, they will be brought face-to-face with the choice to follow Jesus. But the readiness of the unconverted person to receive Jesus and to follow Jesus in the rite of conversion will vary. Once a person has confessed his or her faith and begun the walk into a deeper relationship with Jesus, the steps that person takes are ordered by the meditations designed for each stage.

The discipling stage based on *Be My Disciple!* contains nine meditations dealing with the new believer's relationship to the church, place in worship, and reading and praying of Scripture. The next stage, that of equipping the new Christian in the Spirit, is based on six scriptural meditations found in *Walk in the Spirit!* In these meditations, the maturing Christian is introduced to spiritual warfare, to prayer, and to the essence of the faith summarized in the Apostles' Creed. Finally, the fourth stage of spiritual exposure and growth, based on *Find Your Gift!* studies scriptures that incorporates the new Christian into the full life of the church as the new member discerns his or her gifts, learns what it means to be a steward of creation, is challenged to become a witness, and learns more of what it means to be a eucharistic Christian. These studies occur over seven weeks.

If the three stages of spiritual growth—discipleship, equipping, and incorporating—follow the meditations one week at a time, the total number of weeks is twenty-two, which is nearly six months. This is the *fastest* one can go through the journey. Some converting people may need more time—a year, perhaps two or three. Consequently, the time factor needs to be determined by each congregation and may even vary from person to person. The last thing you want to do is to race through the journey creating immature Christians who have simply "gone through the process." The journey must be authentic and real. Getting through it is not the object; the goal is real and lasting formation of Christian faith and character. For this reason the matter of time must be flexible and related to the growth of the person.

Phase I – Evangelizing the Seeker (Indefinite)	Phase II – Discipling the Hearer (Nine weeks)	Phase III – Equipping the Kneeler (Six weeks)	Phase IV – Incorporating the New Faithful (Seven weeks)
Follow Me!:	*Be My Disciple!:*	*Walk in the Spirit!:*	*Find Your Gift!:*
Based on Scriptural meditations that can be flexed over a period as long as it takes for the seeker to come to a converting decision. This period ends with the Rite of Conversion.	Based on nine Scriptural readings that generally take place over a nine-week period ending with the Rite of Covenant.	Based on six Scriptural lessons and ends with the Rite of Baptism.	Based on seven Scripture studies. The rite connected with this phase is the Eucharist which is continuous.

What Type of External Structure Is Needed for the *Journey to Jesus*?

The next step is to think through the kind of organizing principle you will use for the converting persons who are on the *Journey to Jesus*. There are several possibilities.

First, *Journey to Jesus* may be organized around the one-on-one approach in which the time factor is dependent solely upon the progress of the individual. The one-on-one commitment places the major responsibility on the spiritual mentor who sees the converting person through each stage of development. The disadvantage of this approach is the loss of community that can be fostered in the small group. The advantage is in the flexibility it provides for each new converting person. In the one-on-one approach, the congregation may find itself celebrating the passage rites frequently if new people are continually brought into the process. It might be wise to pace the passage rites so that a group of people can participate in them at the same time.

Second, *Journey to Jesus* may be organized around the academic year at times most suitable to the rhythm of the church. For example, summer and part of the fall may be used for evangelism, late fall for discipling, early winter for equipping the kneeler, and spring as the time to incorporate new members in the church. The advantage of this structure is that it works well with the local church's active time. The disadvantage is that it may not fit into the seasons of the Christian year.

Third, *Journey to Jesus* may be ordered around the Christian year. The church year is an appropriate context for the *Journey to Jesus* because it is an extension of weekly worship. While every Sunday service celebrates the birth, death, resurrection, ascension, and second coming of Jesus Christ, the church year extends the celebration of these events over a full year. Consequently, when the various periods and stages of evangelism coincide with the events of the church year, a deeper, more profound sense of the mystery of Christ and the salvation he brings is realized by the converting person.

The cycle may begin with Pentecost Sunday. On this Sunday, in keeping with its meaning, church members who have been called to evangelism are commissioned in a special ceremony. During the summer and fall they evangelize friends and neighbors using *Follow Me!* In Advent, the rite of conversion takes place. Then, the new convert enters the period of discipleship where *Be My Disciple!* is used. The rite of covenant occurs on the first Sunday of Lent. During Lent, the intense time of spiritual formation takes place, using *Walk in the Spirit!* On the Saturday night Easter vigil or Easter Sunday, the candidates are baptized. Finally, during the fifty days of Easter season, nurture takes place and the converts are integrated into the full life of the church using *Find Your Gift!* In this way, the church year orders the internal experience of repentance, conversion, instruction, and incorporation into the life of the church. This cycle involves not only the converting persons but the whole congregation in a process of renewal.

The advantage of using the Christian year as your organizing principle is that it works well with the amount of time and the number of meditations of the booklets. The disadvantage is that the expectation of spiritual growth within each stage gets locked into a fixed time period. If you choose the Christian year as your organizing principle, discernment about each persons spiritual growth will need to be made. You will not want to prematurely carry a person through a passage rite and into the next stage unless that person is spiritually ready. Turning the journey into an outward and mechanized journey defeats its purpose of forming authentic Christians.

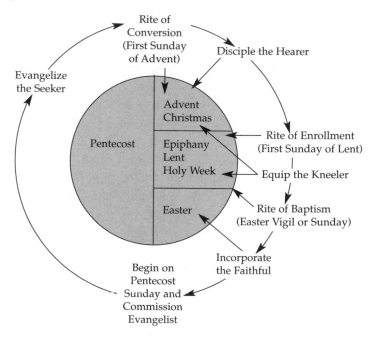

How to Get Started

The *Journey to Jesus* may be used by any church anywhere in the world. It is not complicated, and it can be highly successful when a core of committed people understands it and participates in it.

Your goal is to become a community of worship, evangelism, and nurture. For this reason it is advisable for the entire church or a core community to spend one season going through the process themselves. Choosing to start this way will prove to be enormously beneficial to the church, if there is no current process of evangelism and nurture in place. It will allow the congregation to experiment and to learn as you go; it will renew the congregation and engender enthusiasm. The first go around will give the congregation a sense of the mission and a better grasp of the whole. Here is what a congregation needs to do:

(1) Set up the internal ministry (the pastor of spiritual formation, mentors, and small-group leaders).

(2) Determine the external structure (one-on-one; academic year; Christian year).

(3) Ask for volunteers to go through the process. The rites of passage for the volunteers may be done as "reaffirmation vows," but other than that very little change needs to be made to the *Journey to Jesus*.

Doing the journey *within* the church is particularly beneficial for the congregation that is not currently engaged in an evangelistic and spiritual formation ministry. Some congregations will be ready to do *Journey to Jesus* with a minimum amount of training and in a short period of time. A one-day conference with the leaders and a core of people committed to worship, evangelism, and nurture should be sufficient training to get started.

The benefit of this journey is enormous and has the

potential, when done with prayerful commitment, to reshape the life of the local church and its ministry. It will energize your community, deepen the spirituality of your people and provide a way to do mission that is both authentic and effective.

Leader's Guide

PLANNING A COURSE OF ACTION TO REVI-
TALIZE THE CONGREGATION OR TO REACH
OUT TO THE SEEKER

1. Present the *Journey to Jesus* to your congregation
   or to the core group of people who will make a
   commitment to do the "trial run."
2. Choose the person who will be the pastor of
   spiritual formation, the person who will be the
   worship leader, and those who will be the personal mentors or small-group leaders.
3. Choose the persons who will volunteer to walk
   the *Journey to Jesus*.
4. Now that you have read through *Journey to
   Jesus*, you need to decide how you are going to
   set up the process. Three options have been presented:

   - one-on-one
   - following the academic calendar
   - following the Christian Year

   You are free to create another option. The most
   important factor of your discussion is your
   choice to do it. Don't wait until you have fig-
   ured it all out. Make a commitment to do it and
   work it out as you proceed. *Remember,* you are
   free to make all the adjustments necessary to
   tailor this process to your own tradition and
   situation.

5. Begin. Don't try to fully understand it. Just do
   it. Start with *Follow Me!* and walk through the

entire process, discussing and analyzing it out as you go through each stage. Let the whole church know what you are doing so that they can "see" the process and "sense the journey." Your congregation, and especially those who have passed through the process, will never be the same.

Resources for Further Reading

In order to help churches to start and maintain the *Journey to Jesus* process, the Institute for Worship Studies has created a chat room where people can talk with one another as they are going through the same experience. See *www.instituteforworshipstudies.org*. Click "Discussion," which will lead to the bulletin board for the Worship, Evangelism, and Nurture Mission.

JOURNEY TO JESUS

STAGE	SPIRITUAL GOAL	CONTENT	PASSAGE RITE	RESOURCE
Seeker	Conversion	The gospel	Rite of conversion	*Follow Me!*
Hearer	Discipleship	• Discipled into what it means to be *church* • Discipled into what it means to *worship* • Discipled into how to *read and pray Scripture*	Rite of covenant	*Be My Disciple!*
Kneeler	Equipping	• Equipping for spiritual warfare • Equipping with prayer (the Lord's Prayer) • Equipping with Faith (the Apostles' Creed)	Rite of baptism	*Walk in the Spirit!*
Faithful	Incorporate	• Incorporated into the full life of the church • Discern and use gifts • Stewards of creation • Becoming a witness	The *Eucharist* is the continuous rite of nourishment	*Find Your Gift!*

Notes

1. EVANGELISM OLD AND NEW

1. See Burton Scott Easton, trans. and ed., *The Apostolic Tradition of Hippolytus* (Cambridge: Cambridge University Press, 1934; reprint, Hamden, Conn.: Archon Books, 1962). For a more critical introduction, see Gregory Dix and Henry Chadwick, *The Treatise on the Apostolic Tradition of St. Hippolytus of Rome* (Ridgefield: Morehouse Publishing, 1992).

2. See Murphy Center for Liturgical Research, *Made, Not Born: New Perspectives on Christian Initiation and the Catechumenate* (Notre Dame, Ind.: University of Notre Dame Press, 1976).

3. Michel Dujarier, *The Rites of Christian Initiation* (New York: Sadlier, 1979).

4. Hans-Georg Gadamer, *Truth and Method*, 2d rev. ed., trans. Joel Weinsheimer and Donald G. Marshall (New York: Continuum, 1998).

5. Robert Webber, *Ancient-Future Faith: Rethinking Evangelicalism for a Postmodern World* (Grand Rapids: Baker Books, 1999), p. 30.

6. For postmodern, see Jean-Francois Lyotard, *The Postmodern Condition: A Report on Knowledge* (Minneapolis: University of Minnesota Press, 1997); and Lyotard, *The Postmodern Explained* (Minneapolis: University of Minnesota Press, 1993). For a Christian response to postmodernism, see Stanley J. Grenz, *A Primer on Postmodernism* (Grand Rapids: Eerdmans, 1996); and Webber, *Ancient-Future Faith*. For post-Christian, see Stanley Hauerwas, *After Christendom? How the Church Is to Behave If Freedom, Justice, and a Christian Nation Are Bad Ideas* (Nashville: Abingdon Press, 1991); Stanley Hauerwas and William H. Willimon, *Resident Aliens: Life in the Christian Colony* (Nashville: Abingdon Press, 1989); and Stephen Carter, *The Culture of Disbelief: How American Law and Politics Trivialize Religious Devotion* (New York: HarperCollins, 1993). For neo-pagan, see Christopher Lasch, *The Culture of Narcissism: American Life in an Age of Diminishing Expectations* (New York: W. W. Norton & Company, 1979); Neil Postman, *Amusing Ourselves to Death* (New York: Penguin Books, 1985); and Margot Adler, *Drawing Down the Moon: Witches, Druids, Goddess-Worshippers, and Other Pagans in America Today* (New York: Penguin Books, 1997).

7. John Milbank, *Theology and Social Theory: Beyond Secular Reason*

(Oxford: Blackwell, 1990), p. 383. Milbank and his followers have developed a movement in theology known as "Radical Orthodoxy." See also John Milbank, *The Word Made Strange: Theology, Language, Culture* (Oxford: Blackwell, 1997); John Milbank, Catherine Pickstock and Graham Ward, *Radical Orthodoxy: A New Theology* (New York: Routledge, 1999); and D. Stephen Long, *Divine Economy: Theology and the Market* (New York: Routledge, 2000). This group will be publishing new books each year and promises to be one of the "most talked about" theological trends of the new century.

8. Hauerwas and Willimon, *Resident Aliens*, p. 15. See also Hauerwas, *After Christendom?*

9. See Richard Stark, *The Rise of Christianity: How the Obscure, Marginal Jesus Movement Became the Dominant Religious Force in the Western World in a Few Centuries* (New York: HarperCollins, 1997), esp. ch. 5.

10. Alasdair MacIntyre, *After Virtue: A Study in Moral Theory* (Notre Dame, Ind.: University of Notre Dame Press, 1981).

11. Margot Adler, *Drawing Down the Moon: Witches, Druids, Goddess-Worshippers, and Other Pagans in America Today* (New York: Penguin Books, 1979), p. v.

12. The mission of God is summarized in narrative theology. See Stanley Hauerwas and L. Gregory Jones, *Why Narrative? Readings in Narrative Theology* (Eugene, Ore.: Wipf & Stock Publishers, 1997); and *Hans W. Frei, Theology and Narrative: Selected Essays*, eds. George Hunsinger and William C. Placher (Oxford: Oxford University Press, 1993).

13. See Lesslie Newbigin, *Foolishness to the Greeks: The Gospel and Western Culture* (Grand Rapids: Eerdmans, 1986); David Bosch, *Transforming Mission: Paradigm Shifts in Theology of Mission* (New York: Orbis Books, 1994); Rodney Clapp, *A Peculiar People: The Church as Culture in a Post-Christian Society* (Downers Grove: InterVarsity Press, 1996); George Hunsberger and Craig Van Gelder, *The Church Between Gospel and Culture: The Emerging Mission in North America* (Grand Rapids: Eerdmans, 1996).

14. This form of evangelism has been revived by the Catholic Church and is called the Rites of Christian Initiation for Adults (RCIA). For information, see *Rite of Christian Initiation for Adults: Complete Text of the Rite Together with Additional Rites Approved for Use in the Dioceses of the United States of America* (Chicago: Liturgy Training Publications, 1988). Catholics have taken the ancient resources and adapted them for use in the Roman church. I have drawn from the same resources but have adapted them for the Protestant community. This book draws on my previous study of the origins of this form of evangelism in the third century, *Celebrating Our Faith* (San Francisco: Harper & Row, 1986).

I. THE MISSIONAL CHURCH

2. THE MISSIONAL CHURCH IN THE ANCIENT WORLD

1. The study of Charles Norris Cochrane, *Christianity and Classical Culture* (New York: Oxford University Press, 1944) has not been surpassed.
2. For an elaboration of church-state relations, see Robert M. Grant, *The Sword and the Cross* (New York: Macmillan, 1955).
3. Theophilus, "Letter to Autolycus," 3.15, in *The Ante-Nicene Fathers: Translation of the Writings of the Fathers Down to A.D. 325*, vol. 2 (Grand Rapids: Eerdmans, 1971), p. 115, hereafter cited as ANF.
4. Aristides, *Apology.*
5. Irenaeus, *Against Heresies* 5, as quoted in Webber, *The Church in the World*, p. 53.
6. Irenaeus, *Against Heresies* 4.36, as quoted in Webber, *The Church in the World*, p. 52.
7. Justin Martyr, *First Apology*, as quoted in Webber, *The Church in the World*, p. 52.
8. Ibid.
9. *The Didache* as quoted in Webber, *The Church in the World*, p. 54.
10. See Acts 8:27; 10:1; 13:12; 16:27-34; 18:8; Phil. 4:22; Rom. 6:10-11.
11. Easton, *The Apostolic Tradition of Hippolytus* (Archon), 16 as quoted in Webber, *The Church in the World*, p 54
12. Ibid., as quoted in Webber, *The Church in the World*, p. 54.
13. Tertullian, *On Idolatry* as quoted in Webber, *The Church in the World*, p. 54.
14. Tertullian, *On Shows*, as quoted in Webber, *The Church in the World*, p. 55.
15. Athenagora, *A Plea* as quoted in Webber, *The Church in the World*, p. 54.
16. Lucian, *The Passing of Peregninus* as quoted in Webber, *The Church in the World*, p. 54.
17. Justin Martyr, *Apology* as quoted in Webber, *The Church in the World*, p. 55.
18. Aristides, *Apology* as quoted in Webber, *The Church in the World*, p. 55.
19. *An Epistle to Diognetus* ch. 5, quoted in Cyril Richardson, trans. and ed., *Early Christian Fathers*, The Library of Christian Classics, vol. 1 (Philadelphia: Westminster, 1953), pp. 6-7.
20. See Gustaf Aulén, *Christus Victor*, trans. A. G. Hebert (New York:

Macmillan, 1986); Hendrik Berkhof, *Christ and the Powers* (Scottdale, Penn.: Herald Press, 1977); Gregory A. Boyd, *God at War: The Bible and Spiritual Conflict* (Downers Grove: InterVarsity Press, 1997); Bernard W. Anderson, *From Creation to New Creation: Old Testament Perspectives* (Minneapolis: Fortress Press, 1994); and Georges Florovsky, *Creation and Redemption* (Belmont, Mass.: Nordland Publishing, 1976).

21. G. F. Hawthorne, ed., *Current Issues in Biblical and Patristic Interpretation* (Grand Rapids: Eerdmans, 1975), p. 173.

22. See R. C. D. Jasper and G. J. Cuming, eds., *Prayers of the Eucharist: Early and Reformed*, 2d ed., (New York: Oxford University Press, 1980; 3d ed., Collegeville, Minn.: The Liturgical Press, 1990), pp. 22-23.

23. See Robert Banks, *Paul's Idea of Community: The Early House Churches in Their Historical Setting* (Grand Rapids: Eerdmans, 1980); Carl E. Braaten, *Mother Church: Ecclesiology and Ecumenism* (Minneapolis: Fortress Press, 1998) Dietrich Bonhoeffer, *Life Together* (New York: Harper & Row, 1954); Clapp, *A Peculiar People*; Marva J. Dawn, *Truly the Community: Romans 12 and How to Be the Church* (Grand Rapids: Eerdmans, 1992); Paul D. Hanson, *The People Called: The Growth of Community in the Bible* (New York: Harper & Row, 1986); Stanley Hauerwas, *A Communion of Character: Toward a Constructive Social Ethic* (Notre Dame: University of Notre Dame Press, 1981); and Philip H. Pfatteicher, *The School of the Church: Worship and Christian Formation* (Valley Forge: Trinity Press International, 1995), Grand Rapids: Eerdmans, 1992. For further development of the "church as mother" theme among the early church fathers, see Michel Dujarier, "A Survey of the History of the Catechumanate," in *Becoming a Catholic Christian*, ed. William J. Reedy (New York: Sadlier, 1981), 19ff.

24. Tertullian, *On Martyrdom*, 1, in ANF, vol. 3, p. 693.

25. Clement, *The Instructor*, 1.6, in ANF, vol. 2, p. 220.

26. Cyprian, *Unity of the Church*, 5, in ANF, vol. 5, p. 423.

27. Justin Martyr, *First Apology*, 61, in ANF, vol. 1, p. 183.

28. An excellent expansion of this whole theme is found in Tertullian, *On Baptism*, in ANF, vol. 3, pp. 669-79.

29. Augustine, *The Letters of Petilian, the Donatist*, 3.9–10, in *The Nicene and Post-Nicene Fathers* (Grand Rapids: Eerdmans, 1957) vol. 4, p. 601. Hereafter referred as PNF. Edited by Philip Schaff.

30. Augustine, *Against Donatists*, 1.15-23, in PNF, vol. 4, p. 421.

31. Irenaeus, *Against Heresies*, 4.38.2-3, in *The Early Christian Fathers*, ed. and trans. Henry Bettenson (Oxford: Oxford University Press, 1969), p. 68.

32. Ibid., 2.22.4, in Bettenson, *The Early Christian Fathers*, p. 80.

33. For an extended argument on the incarnational principle that external rites shape internal experience, see Aidan Nichols, O.P., *The Art*

of God Incarnate: Theology and Symbol from Genesis to the Twentieth Century (New York: Paulist Press, 1980).

3. THE MISSIONAL CHURCH TODAY

1. Lyotard, *Postmodern Condition*, p. xxiv.

2. An excellent study on the demise of modernity and the rise of postmodernity is found in Lawrence Cahoone, ed., *From Modernism to Postmodernism: An Anthology* (Oxford: Blackwell, 1996). A helpful historical study is Jacques Barzun, *From Dawn to Decadence: 1500 to the Present* (New York: HarperCollins, 2000); and Paul Johnson, *The Birth of the Modern: World Society 1815–1830* (New York: HarperCollins, 1991).

3. Harold O. J. Brown, *The Sensate Culture: Western Civilization Between Chaos and Transformation* (Dallas: Word Publishing, 1996).

4. Hauerwas and Willimon, *Resident Aliens*, p. 32.

5. See Hauerwas, *After Christendom?*

6. Lesslie Newbigin, *The Open Secret: Sketches for a Missionary Theology* (Grand Rapids: Eerdmans, 1978).

7. Bosch, *Transforming Mission*. Bosch argues for a recovery of the church as mission because this matter "affects the entire church, indeed the entire world" (p. 3).

8. Hunsberger and Van Gelder, *The Church Between Gospel and Culture.* They write: "The social function the churches once fulfilled in American life is gone" (p. xiii).

9. Ibid., p.15.

10. Ibid.

11. Hauerwas, *After Christendom?* p. 36.

12. Ibid.

13. Clapp, *A Peculiar People*, p. 77.

14. Hunsberger and Van Gelder, *The Church Between Gospel and Culture*, p. 17.

15. Vinoth Ramachandra, *The Recovery of Mission: Beyond the Pluralist Paradigm* (Grand Rapids: Eerdmans, 1996), p. 226.

16. Hunsberger and Van Gelder, *The Church Between Gospel and Culture*, p. 22. See also Donald C. Posterski, *Reinventing Evangelism: New Strategies for Presenting Christ in Today's World* (Downers Grove: InterVarsity Press, 1989).

17. Ibid.

18. For a theological exposition of this view based on the writings of the early church fathers see especially Florovsky, *Creation and Redemption*. See also T. F. Torrance, *Theology in Reconciliation: Essays Towards Evangelical and Catholic Unity in East and West* (Grand Rapids: Eerdmans, 1975); and Webber, *Ancient-Future Faith*.

19. See Ramachandra, *Recovery of Mission*, p. 229.

20. Hunsberger and Van Gelder, *The Church Between Gospel and Culture*, p. 22.

21. Ibid., p. 23.

22. Ibid.

23. Aulén, *Christus Victor*, p. 20.

24. Walter Wink, *Naming the Powers*: The Language of Power in the New Testament (Philadelphia: Fortress Press, 1984); *Unmasking the Powers: The Invisible Forces That Determine Human Existence* (Philadelphia: Fortress Press, 1986); *Engaging the Powers: Discernment and Resistance in a World of Domination* (Minneapolis: Fortress Press, 1992); Hendrik Berkhof, John H. Yoder, trans., *Christ and the Powers* (Scottdale: Penn.: Herald Press, 1997); Boyd, *God at War*.

25. Henri de Lubac, *The Christian Faith: The Structure of the Apostles' Creed* (London: Geoffrey Chapman, 1986), as quoted in Braaten, *Mother Church*, p. 3. For other pertinent works on the church, see Bonhoeffer, *Life Together*; Clapp, *A Peculiar People*; Dawn, *Truly the Community*; Hanson, *The People Called*; Hauerwas, *A Communion of Character*; and Pfatteicher, *The School of the Church*.

26. Craig Van Gelder, *The Essence of the Church: A Community Created by the Spirit* (Grand Rapids: Baker Books, 2000), pp. 14-15.

27. James W. Fowler, *The Stages of Faith: The Psychology of Human Development and the Quest for Meaning* (San Francisco: HarperSanFrancisco, 1981).

28. James W. Fowler, *Becoming Adult, Becoming Christian: Adult Development and Christian Faith* (San Francisco: Jossey-Bass Publishers, 2000), p. 10.

29. See Thomas H. Groome, *Christian Religious Education as a Spiritual Journey* (San Francisco: HarperSanFrancisco, 1991); and Parker J. Palmer, *To Know as We Are Known: Education as Spiritual Journey* (San Francisco: HarperSanFrancisco, 1993).

30. Peter Roche de Coppens, *The Nature and Use of Ritual: The Great Christian Documents and Traditional Blue Prints for Human and Spiritual Growth* (Washington, D.C.: University Press of America, 1979), p. 138.

31. Tom F. Driver, *The Magic of Ritual: Our Need for Liberating Rites That Transform Our Lives and Our Communities* (San Francisco: HarperSanFrancisco, 1991), p. 132.

32. Lesslie Newbigin, *The Finality of Christ* (Richmond, Va.: John Knox Press, 1969), p. 96. Quoted in Hunsberger and Van Gelder, *The Church Between Gospel and Culture*, p. 11.

II. EVANGELIZING THE SEEKER

4. EVANGELISM IN THE ANCIENT WORLD

1. Michael Green, *Evangelism in the Early Church* (Grand Rapids: Eerdmans, 1970), p. 48.
2. Ibid., p. 51.
3. Ibid.
4. Ibid.
5. Ibid., p. 53.
6. Ibid., p. 56.
7. Ibid.
8. Ibid., p. 57.
9. Ibid., p. 60.
10. Ibid., p. 56.
11. See ch. 8, "Evangelistic Methods," ibid., pp. 194-235.
12. Stark, *The Rise of Christianity*, p. 3.
13. Ibid., pp. 61-69.
14. Ibid., pp. 73-94.
15. Ibid., p. 161.
16. Ibid., p. 119.
17. Ibid., p. 97.
18. Ibid.
19. Ibid., p. 95.
20. Ibid., p. 178.
21. Ibid.
22. E. R. Dodds, *Pagan and Christian in an Age of Anxiety* (New York: Norton, [1965] 1970), pp. 136-37. Quoted by Stark in *The Rise of Christianity*, p. 207.
23. For early church sources, see Michel Dujarier, *The Rites of Christian Initiation: Historical and Pastoral Reflections* (New York: Sadlier, 1979).
24. Justin Martyr, *The First Apology*, 67, in Richardson, *The Early Christian Fathers*. (See also Easton, *The Apostolic Tradition of Hippolytus*, p. 43).
25. Below is the full text of the ancient inquiry. The vocational demand must be understood in terms of the allegiance occupations demanded to Caesar as Lord. Other vocations to which the church took a dim view infringed on Christian ethics.

New converts to the faith, who are to be admitted as hearers of the word, shall first be brought to the teachers before the people assemble. And they shall be examined as to their reason for embracing the faith, and they who bring them shall testify that they are competent to hear the word. Inquiry shall then be made as to the nature of their life; whether a man has a wife or is a slave. If he is the slave of a believer and he has his master's permission, then let him be received. . . . If his master is a heathen, let the slave be taught to please his master, that the word be not blasphemed. If a man has a wife or a woman a husband, let the man be instructed to content himself with his wife and the woman to content herself with her husband. But if a man is unmarried, let him be instructed to abstain from impurity, either by lawfully marrying a wife or else by remaining as he is. But if any man is possessed with demons, he shall not be admitted as a hearer until he is cleansed.

Inquiry shall likewise be made about the professions and trades of those who are brought to be admitted to the faith. If a man is a pander, he must desist or be rejected. If a man is a sculptor or painter, he must be charged not to make idols; if he does not desist he must be rejected. If a man is an actor or pantomimist, he must desist or be rejected. A teacher of young children had best desist, but if he has no other occupation, he may be permitted to continue. A charioteer, likewise, who races or frequents races, must desist or be rejected. A gladiator or a trainer of gladiators, or a huntsman [in the wild-beast shows], or anyone connected with these shows, or a public official in charge of gladiatorial exhibitions must desist or be rejected. A heathen priest or anyone who tends idols must desist or be rejected. A soldier of the civil authority must be taught not to kill men and to refuse to do so if he is commanded, and to refuse to take an oath; if he is unwilling to comply, he must be rejected. A military commander or civic magistrate that wears the purple must resign or be rejected. If a catechumen or a believer seeks to become a soldier, they must be rejected, for they have despised God. A harlot or licentious man or one who has castrated himself, or any other who does things not to be named, must be rejected, for they are defiled. A magician must not [even] be brought for examination. An enchanter, an astrologer, a diviner, a soothsayer, a user of magic verses, a juggler, a mountebank, an amulet-maker must desist or be rejected. A concubine, who is a slave and has reared her children and has been faithful to her master alone, may become a hearer; but if she has failed in these matters she must be rejected. If a man has a concubine, he must desist and marry legally; if he is unwilling, he must be rejected.

If now, we have omitted anything (any trade?), the facts [as they occur] will instruct your mind; for we all have the Spirit of God. (Easton, *The Apostolic Tradition of Hippolytus*, 2.16, pp. 41-43.
26. Ibid.

5. EVANGELISM TODAY

1. To understand the missional church, see Hunsberger and Van Gelder, *The Church Between Gospel and Culture*, p. 18. The quotes are from Hauerwas and Willimon, *Resident Aliens*.
2. Eddie Gibbs, *ChurchNext: Quantum Changes in How We Do Ministry* (Downers Grove: InterVarsity Press, 2000).
3. Ibid., p. 11.
4. Ibid.
5. Writings not already mentioned that express the priority of a theological understanding of the church include Darrell L. Guder, *Missional Church: A Vision for the Sending of the Church in North America* (Grand Rapids: Eerdmans, 1998); Carl F. Braaten and Robert J. Jenson, ed., *Marks of the Body of Christ* (Grand Rapids: Eerdmans, 1999); Darrell L. Gruder, *The Continuing Conversion of the Church* (Grand Rapids: Eerdmans, 2000); Thomas F. Torrance, *Conflict & Agreement in the Church*, 2 vols. (Eugene, Ore.: Wipf & Stock Publishers, 1959); and Geoffrey Preston, O.P., *Faces of the Church: Meditations on a Mystery and Its Images* (Edinburgh: T & T Clark Ltd., 1997).
6. Inagrace T. Dietterich, "A Particular People: Toward a Faithful and Effective Ecclesiology," in Hunsberger and Van Gelder, *Church Between Gospel and Culture*, p. 348.
7. Roy M. Oswald and Speed B. Leas, *The Inviting Church: A Study in New Member Assimilation* (New York: The Alban Institute, 1987), p. 17.
8. Ibid.
9. Ibid., p. 18.
10. Ibid., pp. 18-19.
11. Christine Pohl, *Making Room: Recovering Hospitality as a Christian Tradition* (Grand Rapids: Eerdmans, 1999), p. x.
12. Ibid.
13. Catching the message through hospitality is by no means a new idea. George Hunter III shows us that hospitality evangelism goes back to the early church. He writes: "The Celtic model for reaching people: (1) You *first* establish community with people, or bring them into the fellowship of your community of faith. (2) Within fellowship, you engage in conversation, ministry, prayer, and worship. (3) In time, as they discover that they now believe, you invite them to commit" (*The Celtic Way of Evangelism* [Nashville: Abingdon Press, 2000], p. 53).
14. "What Teens Believe," May 8, 2000, p. 53 ff.
15. Jean Vanier, *Community and Growth*, (New York: Paulist Press, 1989), p. 8.
16. Oswald and Leas, *The Inviting Church*, p. 28.
17. *Follow Me!* (Wheaton, Ill.: IWS Resources, 2001).

18. Stark, *The Rise of Christianity*.

19. Oswald and Leas, *The Inviting Church*, p. 29.

20. Ibid.

21. Lesslie Newbigin, *The Finality of Christ* (Great Britain: SCM Press, 1969), p. 115.

6. THE RITE OF CONVERSION

1. See *Victor Turner, The Ritual Process: Structure and Antistructure* (Chicago: Aldine Publishing House, 1969). Also see Lionel L. Mitchell, *The Meaning of Ritual* (Grand Rapids: Eerdmans, 1973).

2. Easton, *The Apostolic Tradition of Hippolytus*, p. 41.

3. Origen, *Against Celsus*, 3.51, in *The Ancient-Nicene Fathers*, vol. 4, ed. A. Cleveland Coxe (Grand Rapids: Eerdmans, 1972), p. 484.

4. See Michel Dujarier, *The Rites of Christian Initiation* (New York: Sadlier, 1979), pp. 35-39.

5. See "History of the Catechumanate," in ibid., pp. 19-26. The rite of entrance is reconstructed from biblical and early church sources. Since there is no mention of the rite of entrance in the New Testament, we acknowledge it to be a creation of the church. However, it is based on biblical principles.

6. Regis A. Duffy, O.F.M., *On Becoming a Catholic: The Challenge of Christian Initiation* (San Francisco: Harper & Row, 1984), p. 86.

III. DISCIPLING THE HEARER

INTRODUCTION

1. Walter Henrichsen, *Disciples Are Made, Not Born* (Colorado Springs: Cook Communications, 1988), p. 10.

7. DISCIPLESHIP IN THE ANCIENT CHURCH

1. See Philip Carrington, *The Primitive Christian Catechism* (Cambridge: The University Press, 1940), pp. 42-43.

2. Easton, *The Apostolic Tradition*, p. 41. Here is the text of Hippolytus: "Let catechumens spend three years as hearers of the word. But if a man is zealous and perseveres well in the work, it is not the time but his character that is decisive" (2.17, in ibid., p. 43).

3. Justin Martyr, *The First Apology*, 67, in Richardson, *Early Christian Fathers*, p. 287.

8. DISCIPLESHIP TODAY

1. Fowler, *Becoming Adult, Becoming Christian*, p. vii.
2. Ibid., pp. 2-6.
3. Ibid., p. 8.
4. Ibid., p. 10.
5. Francis Kelly Nemeck and Marie Theresa Coombs, *The Way of Spiritual Direction* (Collegeville, Minn.: Liturgical Press, 1985), pp. 13-14.
6. Robert Wuthnow, *"I Come Away Stronger": How Small Groups Are Shaping American Religion* (Grand Rapids: Eerdmans, 1994), p. 2. See also Gareth Weldon Icenogle, *Biblical Foundations for Small Group Ministry: An Integrational Approach* (Downers Grove: InterVarsity Press, 1994).
7. Wuthnow, *"I Come Away Stronger,"* pp. 344-45.
8. Palmer, *To Know as We Are Known*, p. xii.
9. Ibid., p. xv.
10. *Be My Disciple!*
11. See James W. Carey, *Communication as Culture: Essays on Media and Society* (New York: Routledge, 1992). See also James J. O'Donnell, *Avatars of the Word: From Papyrus to Cyberspace* (Cambridge: Harvard University Press, 1998); and Pierre Babin, *New Era of Religious Education* (Minneapolis: Fortress Press, 1991), esp. ch. 1, "Religious Education from Gutenberg to the Electronic Age." See the seminal work of Mircea Eliade, *Myth and Reality* (New York: Harper & Row, 1963); and the more recent work of Catherine Bell, *Ritual Theory, Ritual Practice* (New York: Oxford University Press, 1992); and Driver, *Magic of Ritual.*
12. Two books that are helpful in guiding the local church toward the experience of community are Larry Crabb, *The Safest Place on Earth* (Nashville: Word Publishing, 1999); and Dawn, *Truly the Community.*
13. For an excellent discussion on the relationship between evangelism and community, see Vanier, *Community and Growth.*
14. Clapp, *A Peculiar People*, p. 82.
15. Willard Swartley and Donald Kraybill, *Building Communities of Compassion: Mennonite Mutual Aid in Theory and Practice* (Herald, 1999), pp. 15-16.
16. See the writings of Marva Dawn, esp. *A Royal "Waste" of Time: The Splendor of Worshiping God and Being Church for the World* (Grand Rapids: Eerdmans, 1999).
17. See the eucharistic prayer of Hippolytus, *The Apostolic Tradition*, 4.11, in Jasper and Cuming, *Prayers of the Eucharist*, p. 23.
18. See Robert E. Webber, *Worship Is a Verb* (Peabody: Hendrickson, 1985).

19. Thelma Hall, R.C., *Too Deep for Words: Rediscovering Lectio Divina* (New York: Paulist Press, 1988), p. 9.
20. Ibid., p. 20.
21. Ibid. This section is an abbreviated version from the original text (pp. 36-55).
22. Ibid., p. 44.

9. THE RITE OF COVENANT

1. See Easton, *Apostolic Tradition of Hippolytus*, p. 44.
2. See Edward Yarnold, S.J., ed., *The Awe-Inspiring Rites of Initiation: Baptismal Homilies of the Fourth Century* (London: St. Paul Publications, 1972).

IV. EQUIPPING THE KNEELER

10. SPIRITUAL FORMATION IN THE ANCIENT CHURCH

1. For reflection on the warfare theme in prebaptismal instruction, see Carrington, *The Primitive Christian Catechism*.
2. For a biblical description of the conflict of God with evil, see Boyd, *God at War.*
3. To understand how intense this battle between good and evil is understood to be in the ancient church, see *Unseen Warfare*, as edited by Nicodemus of the Holy Mountain and revised by Theophan the Recluse (Crestwood, N.Y.: St. Vladimir's Seminary Press, 1995). For a historical overview of the subject, see Aulén, *Christus Victor*; and Jeffrey Burton Russell, *The Prince of Darkness: Radical Evil and the Power of Good in History* (Ithaca, N.Y.: Cornell University Press, 1988).
4. Here is the text of Hippolytus regarding the exorcisms of prayers:

Then from the time that they are separated from the other catechumens, hands shall be laid upon them daily in exorcism and, as the day of their baptism draws near, the bishop himself shall exorcise each one of them that he may be personally assured of their purity. Then, if there is any of them who is not good or pure, he shall be put aside as not having heard the word in faith; for it is never possible for the alien to be concealed. (Easton, *The Apostolic Tradition of Hippolytus*, p. 44)

5. Quoted by Dujarier, *The Rites of Christian Initiation*, p. 121.

6. Easton, *The Apostolic Tradition of Hippolytus*, pp. 44-45.
7. Anne Field, O.S.B., *From Darkness to Light: How One Became a Christian in the Early Church* (Ben Lomond, Calif.: Conciliar Press, 1997), pp. 83-86.
8. Quoted by Dujarier, *The Rites of Christian Initiation*, p. 139.
9. Ibid., p. 140.
10. Ibid., p. 139.
11. Ibid., p. 141.
12. Ibid., p. 134.

11. SPIRITUAL FORMATION TODAY

1. Joseph J. Allen, *Inner Way: Toward a Rebirth of Eastern Christian Spiritual Direction* (Grand Rapids: Eerdmans, 1994), p. ix.
2. See MacIntyre, *After Virtue*.
3. Eugene H. Peterson, *Subversive Spirituality* (Grand Rapids: Eerdmans, 1997), p. ix.
4. Ranald Macaulay and Jerram Barrs, *Being Human: The Nature of Spiritual Experience* (Downers Grove: InterVarsity Press, 1978), p. 16.
5. Dallas Willard, *The Spirit of the Disciplines: Understanding How God Changes Lives* (San Francisco: HarperSanFrancisco, 1991), p. ix.
6. The phrase "a long obedience in the same direction" originated with Nietzsche and has been used as a title for a book by Eugene H. Peterson, *A Long Obedience in the Same Direction: Discipleship in an Instant Society* (Downers Grove: InterVarsity, 1980).
7. Boyd, *God at War*. Numerous books have been written on spiritual warfare. Among the more recent are Walter Wink, *Naming the Powers: The Language of Power in the New Testament* (Philadelphia: Fortress Press, 1984); *Unmasking the Powers: The Invisible Forces That Determine Existence* (Philadelphia: Fortress Press, 1986); *Engaging the Powers* (Philadelphia: Fortress Press, 1992); Calvin Miller, *Disarming the Darkness : A Guide to Spiritual Warfare* (Grand Rapids: Zondervan, 1998); Ed Murphy, *The Handbook for Spiritual Warfare* (Nashville: Thomas Nelson, 1992); and A. Scott Moreau, *Essential of Spiritual Warfare: Equipped to Win the Battle* (Wheaton, Ill.: Harold Shaw, 1997).
8. *Didache* 2, 3, 5; see Richardson, *Early Christian Fathers*, pp. 172-74.
9. Each church should adapt the following three sets of prayers to their own setting:

(1) The spiritual mentors place their hands on kneelers' heads, shoulders, or backs while the leader prays.
(2) The minister invites the people to join in prayer for the kneelers as they prepare for baptism.

(3) The minister intercedes for the kneelers. The people may respond with an *Amen* or *Lord hear our prayer* at the end of each prayer.

INTERCESSIONS

(For each week of prayers, choose several of the following themes.)
- That they may read, study, learn and follow the Scripture
- That they may know Christ as Savior
- That they may confess themselves as sinners so that they may turn from sin
- That the Holy Spirit may teach them the things of God
- That they may become true worshipers of God
- That they may be thankful for the work of God in Jesus Christ
- That they may grow in holiness
- That they may become Christlike
- That they may be filled with hope
- That they may share the good news with others
- That they may remain faithful to the teachings of Jesus
- That God may bring healing into their lives

THE PRAYER OF EXORCISM

(Pray with out stretched hands, using the following themes:)

- That they may be aware of the evil powers
- That they may enjoy freedom from sin
- That God will crush the powers of Satan
- That God will protect from all temptations
- That they will deal with hidden sin
- That Christ may rule over all sin
- That they may experience deliverance from the spirit of lust, envy, hate greed, covetousness, malice, jealousy, greed, and unbridled ambition
- That they may be freed from false values
- That they may stand firmly in your truth
- That they may live as children of the light
- That they may trust in the truth of Christ
- That they may seek the things that are just and holy
- That they may experience healing
- That their faith may be strengthened

For more extended prayers, see *The Rites of the Catholic Church* (New York: Pueblo, 1983), pp. 152-207.

10. Johannes A. van der Ven, *Formation of the Moral Self* (Grand Rapids: Eerdmans, 1998), pp. 189-99.

11. Anne Field, *From Darkness to Light: How One Became a Christian in the Early Church* (Ben Lomond: Conciliar Press, 1997), p. 60.

12. Don E. Saliers, *The Soul in Paraphrase: Prayer and the Religious Affections* (Cleveland: OSL Publications, 1991), pp. 97-98.

13. Dallas Willard, *The Divine Conspiracy: Rediscovering Our Hidden Life in God* (San Francisco: HarperSanFrancisco, 1998), p. 269.

14. Presentation of the creed
- The kneelers are invited to come forward
- The pastor reminds them that the creed is the summary of Christian faith. It should be memorized and repeated daily for it is the guardian of the truth, a power against false understandings of the world
- The creed is said by all:

I believe in God, the Father almighty,
creator of heaven and earth.
I believe in Jesus Christ, his only Son, our Lord.
He was conceived by the power of the Holy Spirit
And born of the Virgin Mary.
He suffered under Pontius Pilate,
Was crucified, died, and was buried.
He descended to the dead.
On the third day he rose again.
He ascended into heaven,
And is seated at the right hand of the Father.
He will come again to judge the living and the dead.
I believe in the Holy Spirit,
The holy catholic Church,
The communion of saints,
The forgiveness of sins,
The resurrection of the body,
And the life everlasting. Amen.

- A prayer is said over the kneelers as all stretch their hands toward them in the sign of blessing. The pastor asks God to impress the faith upon them that they may walk *within* it and not see it only as a faith outside of themselves.

15. Presentation of the Lord's Prayer
- The pastor invites the kneelers to come forward
- The pastor admonishes the kneelers on the value of the prayer as a weapon of warfare, a guard against the error of self-sufficiency.

* The prayer is said together

Our Father,
who art in heaven,
hallowed be thy name;
thy kingdom come;
thy will be done on earth
as it is in heaven.
Give us this day our daily bread
And forgive us our trespasses
As we forgive those
Who trespass against us;
And lead us not into temptation,
But deliver us from evil.

* The pastor now prays for the kneelers as the hands of all are out-stretched toward them in a sign of blessing. The pastor prays that they may live *within* the Lord's Prayer, making it real and personal for themselves.

16. See John Meyendorff, *St. Gregory Palamas and Orthodox Spirituality* (Crestwood, N.Y.: St. Vladimir's Seminary Press, 1974), p. 14.

12. THE RITE OF BAPTISM

1. See Justin Martyr, *First Apology*, 65.
2. The text of Hippolytus reads:

> They who are to be baptized shall fast on Friday, and on Saturday the bishop shall assemble them and command them to kneel in prayer. And, laying his hand upon them, he shall exorcise all evil spirits to flee away and never to return; when he has done this he shall breathe in their faces, seal their foreheads, ears and noses, and then raise them up. They shall spend all that night in vigil, listening to reading and instruction. (Easton, *The Apostolic Tradition of Hippolytus*, pp. 44-45)

3. The text reads:

> At cockcrow prayer shall be made over the water. The stream shall flow through the baptismal tank or pour into it from above when there is no scarcity of water; but if there is a scarcity, whether constant or sudden, then use whatever water you can find.
> They shall remove their clothing. And first baptize the little ones; if they can speak for themselves, they shall do so; if not, their parents or other relatives shall speak for them. Then baptize the men,

and last of all the women; they must first loosen their hair and put aside any gold or silver ornaments that they were wearing: let no one take any alien thing down to the water with them. (ibid., p. 45)

4. The text reads:

At the hour set for the baptism the bishop shall give thanks over oil and put it into a vessel: this is called the "oil of thanksgiving." And he shall take other oil and exorcise it: this is called "the oil of exorcism." [The anointing is performed by a presbyter]. A deacon shall bring the oil of exorcism, and shall stand at the presbyter's left hand. . . . Then the presbyter, taking hold of each of those about to be baptized, shall command him to renounce, saying:
I renounce thee, Satan, and all thy servants and all thy works.
And when he has renounced all these, the presbyter shall anoint him with the oil of exorcism, saying:
Let all spirits depart far from thee. (ibid., pp. 45-46)

5. The text of the creed reads:

Then, after these things, let him give over to the presbyter who baptizes, and let the candidates stand in the water, naked, a deacon going with them likewise. And when he who is being baptized goes down into the water, he who baptizes him, putting his hand on him, shall say thus:
Dost thou believe in God, the Father Almighty?
And he who is being baptized shall say:
I believe.
Then holding his hand placed on his head, he shall baptize him once. And then he shall say:
Dost thou believe in Christ Jesus, the Son of God, who was born of the Holy Ghost of the Virgin Mary, and was crucified under Pontius Pilate, and was dead and buried, and rose again the third day, alive from the dead, and ascended into heaven, and sat at the right hand of the Father, and will come to judge the quick and the dead? And when he says:
I believe,
he is baptized again. And again he shall say:
Dost thou believe in [the] Holy Ghost, and the holy church, and the resurrection of the flesh?
He who is being baptized shall say accordingly:
I believe,
and so he is baptized a third time. (ibid., pp. 46-47)

6. The instructions regarding the sealing of the spirit are:

And afterward, when he has come up [out of the water], he is anointed by the presbyter with the oil of thanksgiving, the presbyter saying:
I anoint thee with holy oil in the name of Jesus Christ.
And so each one, after drying himself, is immediately clothed, and then is brought into the church.

Then the bishop, laying his hand upon them, shall pray, saying:
O Lord God, who hast made them worthy to obtain remission of sins through the laver of regeneration of [the] Holy Spirit, send into them thy grace, that they may serve thee according to thy will; for thine is the glory, to the Father and the Son, with [the] Holy Spirit in the holy church, both now and world without end. Amen.
Then, pouring the oil of thanksgiving from his hand and putting it on his forehead, he shall say:
I anoint thee with holy oil in the Lord, the Father Almighty and Christ Jesus and [the] Holy Ghost.
And signing them on the forehead he shall say:
The Lord be with thee;
and he who is signed shall say:
And with thy spirit. (ibid., pp. 47-48)

7. The text reads:

And then the offering is immediately brought by the deacons to the bishop, and by thanksgiving he shall make the bread into an image of the body of Christ, and the cup of wine mixed with water according to likeness of the blood, which is shed for all who believe in him. And milk and honey mixed together for the fulfilment of the promise to the fathers, which spoke of a land flowing with milk and honey; namely, Christ's flesh which he gave, by which they who believe are nourished like babes, he making sweet the bitter things of the heart by the gentleness of his word. And the water into an offering in a token of the laver, in order that the inner part of man, which is a living soul, may receive the same as the body.
The bishop shall explain the reason of all these things to those who partake. And when he breaks the bread and distributes the fragments he shall say:
The heavenly bread in Christ Jesus.
And the recipient shall say, Amen.
And the presbyters—or if there are not enough presbyters, the deacons—shall hold the cups, and shall stand by with reverence and modesty; first he who holds the water, then the milk, thirdly the wine. And the recipients shall taste of each three times, he who gives the cup saying:
In God the Father Almighty;
and the recipient shall say, Amen. Then:
In the Lord Jesus Christ;
[and he shall say, Amen. Then:
In] [the] Holy Ghost and the holy church;
and he shall say, Amen. So it shall be done to each. (ibid., pp. 48-49)

The milk and honey symbolize the hope of Israel for the promised land. Here, in the Christian sense, they symbolize entrance into the church, the promises of salvation, the new birth, and the sweetness of Christ.

These symbols of baptism as described by Hippolytus are clearly modeled on the meaning of baptism in the New Testament. Baptism culminates a process that brings a person into a saving relationship with Jesus Christ. It is not a mere formality, but a genuine path toward a relationship that will be nurtured in the church.

8. For the great paschal vigil, see Robert Webber, ed., *The Services of the Christian Year,* The Complete Library of Christian Worship, vol. 5 (Peabody: Hendrickson, 1994), pp. 383-95.

V. INCORPORATING THE FAITHFUL: RECEIVING THE NEW MEMBER

13. RECEIVING NEW MEMBERS IN THE ANCIENT CHURCH

1. The text of Hippolytus, *The Apostolic Tradition* reads:

> And when these things are completed, let each one hasten to do good works, and to please God and to live aright, devoting himself to the church, practising the things he has learned, advancing in the service of God.
>
> Now we have briefly delivered to you these things concerning holy baptism and the holy oblation, for you have already been instructed concerning the resurrection of the flesh and all other things as taught in Scripture. Yet if there is any other thing that ought to be told [to converts], let the bishop impart it to them privately after their baptism; let not unbelievers know it, until they are baptized: this is the white stone of which John said: "There is upon it a new name written, which no one knoweth but he that receiveth the stone." (Easton, *The Apostolic Tradition of Hippolytus,* p. 49)

2. Justin Martyr, *First Apology,* in Richardson, *Early Christian Fathers,* pp. 285-86.

3. Justin Martyr, *First Apology,* 65.

4. The text reads:

> May all actions and all words be turned toward God. Bring all your concerns to Christ, and at every instant, turn your soul toward God. Base all your reflection solidly on the power of Christ, so that it may rest calmly, sheltered from the waves of all needless talk and agitation, in the divine light of the Savior. Day after day, share your thinking with men, but join it to that of God, during the day as well as at night. Do not let yourself fall into a deep sleep which closes your eyes and deadens your mind to prayers and hymns, for this kind of sleep is a prelude to death. Keep yourself always in active union with Christ who sends you from heaven his brilliant light. May Christ be your constant and unending joy. (Quoted from Dujarier, *Rites of Christian Initiation,* p. 211)

5. Cyril of Jerusalem captured the meaning of the white robes in the lectures he gave in Jerusalem in the fourth century.

> Now that you have divested yourself of your former clothes and have clothed yourselves in spiritual white ones, you must always be clothed in white. By no means do we want you to understand by this that your clothes must always be white; but that you must be clothed with true whiteness and with spiritual splendor, so that you may say with blessed Isaiah: "My soul rejoices in the Lord, for he has clothed me with the garment of salvation and has wrapped me in a tunic of joy." (Quoted by Dujarier, *Rites of Christian Initiation*, p. 214)

6. Quoted by Dujarier, ibid., p. 215.
7. U.S. Catholic Conference, *RCIA*, 38.
8. Quoted by Dujarier, ibid., p. 213.

14. RECEIVING NEW MEMBERS TODAY

1. Van Gelder, *Essence of the Church*, p. 153.
2. Pohl, *Making Room*, p. x.
3. Greg Ogden, *The New Reformation: Returning the Ministry to the People of God* (Grand Rapids: Zondervan, 1990), p. 117ff.
4. Ibid., p. 52ff.
5. Ibid., p. 130, quoted from Elizabeth O'Conner, *Eighth Day of Creation*.
6. Ibid., p. 97, quoted from Elton Trueblood, *The Incendiary Fellowship* (New York: Harper & Row, 1967), p. 41.
7. R. Paul Stevens, *Liberating the Laity: Equipping All the Saints for Ministry* (Vancouver: Regent College Publishing, 1993).
8. Melvin J. Steinbron, *The Lay-Driven Church: How to Empower the People in Your Church to Share the Tasks of Ministry* (Ventura, Calif.: Regal, 1997), p. 165.
9. Paul Lakeland, *Postmodernity: Christian Identity in a Postmodern Age* (Minneapolis: Fortress Press. 1997), p. 46.
10. Vigen Guroian, *Ethics After Christendom: Toward an Ecclesial Christian Ethic* (Grand Rapids: Eerdmans, 1994), p. 159.
11. Ibid., p. 160.

15. THE RITE OF EUCHARIST

1. Jasper and Cuming, *Prayers of the Eucharist*, pp. 22-23.
2. A very helpful book on the philosophy of eating is Leon R. Kass, M.D., *The Hungry Soul: Eating and the Perfecting of Our Nature* (Chicago: University Press, 1999).

Bibliography

Primary Sources

Ambrose
On the Mysteries and *Treatise on the Sacraments.* Translated by T. Thompson. Edited by J.H. Strawley. London: SPCK, 1919.
Des Sacrements, Des Mysteres, l'Explication du Symbole. Edited by B. Botte. Sources Chretiennes, 25 bis. Paris: Editions du Cerf, 1961.

Augustine
Sermons. Edited by J. P. Migne. Patrologia Latina, 38, 39, 40, 46. *Sermons pour la Pacque.* Edited by S. Poque. Sources Chretiennes, 116. Paris: Editions du Cerf, 1966.
First Catechetical Instruction. Translated by J. P. Christopher. Ancient Christian Writers, 2. Westminster, Md.: Newman Press, 1946.

Chromatius
Sermons. Edited by J. Lemaire. Sources Chretiennes, 154. Paris: Editions du Cerf, 1969.

John Chrysostom
Huit Catecheses Baptismales. Edited by A. Wenger. Sources Chretiennes, 50 bis. Paris: Editions du Cerf, 1970.

Cyprian
Treatisis. Translated by C. Thornton. Library of the Fathers. Oxford: J. H. Parker, 1899.

Cyril of Jerusalem
The Catechetical Lectures. Edited by W. Telfer. Library of Christian Classics, 4. London: SCM Press, 1965.
St. Cyril of Jerusalem's Lectures on the Christian Sacraments. Edited by F. L. Cross. London: SPCK, 1951.

Egira
Egira's Travel. Edited by J. Wilkinson. London: SPCK, 1971.

Hippolytus
The Apostolic Tradition of Hippolytus. Edited by Burton Scott Easton. Cambridge: Cambridge University Press, 1934.
The Treatise on the Apostolic Tradition of St. Hippolytus of Rome. Edited by Gregory Dix and Henry Chadwick. Ridgefield: London, Morehouse Publishing. Second revised edition, 1947, 1968, 1992.

Quodvultdeus
Sermons on the Creed. Edited by J.P. Migne, Patrologia Latina, 40, 41.

Sarapion
Bishop Sarapion's Prayer Book. Edited by J. Wordsworth. London: SPCK, 1915.

Theodore of Mopsuestia
Les Homelies Catechetiques. Edited by R. Tonneau and R. Devreesse. Rome: Vatican Press, 1949.

Tertullian
Treatise on Baptism. Translated by C. Dodgson. Library of the Fathers. Oxford: J. H. Parker, 1942.

(*For most of the sources above I am indebted to Anne Field, *From Darkness to Light* [Ben Lomond, Calif.: Conciliar Press, 1978].)

Primary Source Collections

Finn, Thomas M. *Early Christian Baptism and the Catechumenate.* Italy, North Africa, and Egypt; Collegeville, Minn.: Liturgical Press.
Whitaker, E. C. *Documents of the Baptismal Liturgy.* London: SPCK; 1960, 1970, 1977, 1985.
Yarnold, Edward S. J. *The Awe-Inspiring Rites of Initiation: Baptismal Homilies of the Fourth Century.* Middlegreen, Slough: St. Paul Publication, 1971.

Booklets for the Journey to Jesus

Follow Me! Wheaton, Ill.: IWS Resources, 2001.
Be My Disciple! Wheaton, Ill.: IWS Resources, 2001.
Walk in the Spirit! Wheaton, Ill.: IWS Resources, 2001.
Find Your Gift! Wheaton, Ill.: IWS Resources, 2001.

Secondary Sources

This select list of secondary sources follows the outline of the book.

INTRODUCTION

Benedict, Dan. *Come to the Waters: Baptism and Our Ministry of Welcoming Seekers and Making Disciples.* Nashville: Upper Room, 1998.

Dujarier, Michel. *The Rites of Christian Initiation.* New York: Sadlier, 1979.

Keifert, Patrick R. *Welcoming the Stranger: A Public Theology of Worship and Evangelism.* Minneapolis: Fortress Press, 1992.

Field, Anne. *From Darkness to Light: How One Became a Christian in the Early Church.* Ben Lomond, Calif.: Conciliar Press, 1978.

Hunter, George. *The Celtic Way of Evangelism: How Christianity Can Reach the West . . . Again.* Nashville: Abingdon Press, 2000.

Murphy Center for Liturgical Research. *Made, Not Born: New Perspectives on Christian Initiation and the Catechumenate.* Notre Dame, Ind.: University of Notre Dame Press, 1976. Office of Evangelism Ministries, The Episcopal Church. *The Catechumenical Process: Adult Initiation for Christian Life and Ministry.* New York: The Church Hymnal Corporation, 1990.

Senn, Frank C. *The Witness of the Worshiping Community: Liturgy and the Practice of Evangelism.* Mahwah, N.J.: Paulist Press, 1993.

Turner, Paul. *The Hallelujah Highway: A History of the Catechumenate.* Chicago: Liturgy Training Publication, 2000.

Postmodern

Gadamer, Hans-Georg. *Truth and Method.* New York: Continuum, 1998. Second revised edition.

Grenz, Stanley J. *A Primer on Postmodernism.* Grand Rapids: Eerdmans, 1996.

Lyotard, Jean Francois. *The Postmodern Condition: A Report on Knowledge.* Minneapolis: University of Minnesota Press, 1984.

———. *The Post Modern Explained: Correspondence 1982–1985.* Minneapolis: University of Minneapolis Press, 1993.

Post-Christian

Barzun, Jacques. *From Dawn to Decadence: Five Hundred Years of Cultural Life: 1500 to the Present.* New York: HarperCollins Publishers, 2000.

Carson, D. A. *The Gagging of God: Christianity Confronts Pluralism.* Grand Rapids: Zondervan, 1996.

Carter, Stephen. *The Culture of Disbelief: How American Law and Politics Trivialize Religious Devotion*. New York: HarperCollins Publishers, 1993.

Hauerwas, Stanley. *After Christendom? How the Church Is to Behave If Freedom, Justice, and a Christian Nation Are Bad Ideas*. Nashville: Abingdon Press, 1991.

Himmelforb, Gertrude. *The De-Moralization of Society: From Victorian Virtues to Modern Values*. New York: Random House, 1996.

Lasch, Christopher. *The Culture of Narcissism: American Life in an Age of Diminishing Expectations*. New York: W. W. Norton & Company, 1979.

Postman, Neal. *Amusing Ourselves to Death: Public Discourse in the Age of Show Business*. New York: Penguin Books, 1985.

Shattuck, Roger. *Candor & Perversion: Literature, Education, and the Arts*. New York: W. W. Norton & Company, 1999.

Stephens, Mitchell. *The Rise of the Image, The Fall of the Word*. New York: Oxford, 1998.

Wuthnow, Robert. *The Struggle for American Soul: Evangelicals, Liberals, and Secularism*. Grand Rapids: Eerdmans, 1992.

_____. *Rediscovering the Sacred: Perspectives on Religion in Contemporary Society*. Grand Rapids: Eerdmans, 1992.

Neo-Pagan

Adler, Margot. *Drawing Down the Moon: Witches, Druids, Goddess-Worshippers, and Other Pagans in America Today*. New York: Penguin Books, 1979, 1986. Revised and expanded edition.

Lehmann, Arthur C. and James E. Myers. *Magic, Witchcraft and Religion: An Anthropological Study of the Supernatural*. Mountain View, Calif.: Mayfield Publishing Company, 1985, 1989. Second edition.

Return to the Early Church

Cutsinger, James (ed.). *Reclaiming the Great Tradition: Evangelicals, Catholics & Orthodox in Dialogue*. Downers Grove: InterVarsity Press, 1997.

Laurence, Paul. *Radical Orthodoxy? A Catholic Inquiry*. Burlington: Ashgate, 2000.

Milbank, John. *Theology and Social Theory: Beyond Secular Reason*. Oxford: Blackwell Publishers, 1990, 1998.

_____. *The Word Made Strange: Theology, Language, Culture.* Oxford: Blackwell Publishers, 1997.

Milbank, John, Catherine Pickstock, and Graham Ward (eds). *Radical Orthodoxy: A New Theology.* London: Routledge, 1999.

Pickstock, Catherine. *After Writing: On the Liturgical Consummation of Philosophy.* Oxford: Blackwell Publishers, 1998, 1999.

Webber, Robert. *Ancient-Future Faith: Rethinking Evangelicalism for a Postmodern World.* Grand Rapids: Baker Books, 1999.

Wilken, Robert L. *Remembering the Christian Past.* Grand Rapids: Eerdmans, 1995.

Williams, D. H. *Retrieving the Tradition and Renewing Evangelism: A Primer for Suspicious Protestants.* Grand Rapids: Eerdmans, 1999.

I. THE MISSIONAL CHURCH

The Missional Church in Pagan Rome

Fox, Robin Lane. *Pagans and Christians.* New York: Alfred A. Knopf Inc., 1987.

Smith, John Holland. *The Death of Classical Paganism.* New York: Charles Scribner's Sons, 1976.

Stark, Rodney. *The Rise of Christianity: How the Obscure, Marginal Jesus Movement Became the Dominant Religious Force in the Western World in a Few Centuries.* New York: HarperCollins, 1997.

The Missional Church in North America Today

Bosch, David. *Transforming Mission: Paradigm Shifts in Theology of Mission.* Maryknoll, N.Y.: Orbis Books, 1994.

Braaten, Carl E. *Mother Church: Ecclesiology and Ecumenism.* Minneapolis: Fortress Press, 1998.

Braaten, Carl E. and Robert W. Jenson. *Marks of the Body of Christ.* Grand Rapids: Eerdmans, 1999.

Clapp, Rodney. *A Peculiar People: The Church as Culture in a Postmodern Society.* Downers Grove: InterVarsity Press, 1996.

Gibbs, Eddie. *ChurchNext: Quantum Changes in How We Do Ministry.* Downers Grove: InterVarsity Press, 2000.

Groff, Ira Kent. *The Soul of Tomorrow's Church: Weaving Spiritual Practices in Ministry Together.* Nashville: Upper Room, 2000.

Guder, Darrell L. (ed.). *Missional Church: A Vision for the Sending of the Church in North America.* Grand Rapids: Eerdmans, 1998.

_____. *The Continuing Conversion of the Church*. Grand Rapids: Eerdmans, 2000.

Hauerwas, Stanley, and William H. Willimon. *Resident Aliens: Life in the Christian Colony*. Nashville: Abingdon Press, 1989.

Hunsberger, George, R. and Craig Van Gelder (eds). *The Church Between Gospel and Culture: The Emerging Mission in North America*. Grand Rapids: Eerdmans, 1996.

McLaren, Brian D. *The Church on the Other Side: Doing Ministry in the Postmodern Matrix* Grand Rapids: Zondervan, 2000.

Ramachandra, Vinoth. *The Recovery of Mission: Beyond the Pluralist Paradigm*. Grand Rapids: Eerdmans, 1996.

Riddell, Michael. *Threshold of the Future: Reforming the Church in the Post-Christian West*. London: SPCK, 1998.

Roxburgh, Alan J. *The Missionary Congregation, Leadership and Liminality*. Harrisburg, Penn.: Trinity Press International, 1997.

Schaller, Lyle E. (ed.). *One Church, Many Congregations: The Key Church Strategy*. Nashville: Abingdon Press, 1999.

Schwarz, Christian A. *Natural Church Development: A Guide to Eight Essential Qualities of Healthy Churches*. Carol Stream, Ill.: Churchsmart, 1998. Third edition.

van der Ven, Johannes A. *Ecclesiology in Context*. Grand Rapids: Eerdmans, 1996.

Vanier, Jean. *Community and Growth*. Mahwah, N.J.: Paulist Press, 1989.

Van Gelder, Craig. *Confident Witness—Changing World: Rediscovering the Gospel in North America*. Grand Rapids: Eerdmans, 1999.

_____. *The Essence of the Church: A Community Created by the Spirit*. Grand Rapids: Baker, 2000.

Warren, Andrew. *Telling the Story: Gospel Mission and Culture*. London: SPCK, 1996.

Warren, Rick. *The Purpose Driven Church: Growth Without Compromising Your Message and Mission*. Grand Rapids: Zondervan, 1995.

PART II — EVANGELIZING THE SEEKER

Evangelizing the Seeker in the Early Church

Green, Michael. *Evangelism in the Early Church*. Grand Rapids: Eerdmans, 1970.

Evangelizing the Seeker Today

Abraham, William. *The Logic of Evangelism*. Grand Rapids: Eerdmans, 1989.

Beaudoin, Tom. *Virtual Faith: The Irreverent Spiritual Quest of Generation X*. San Francisco: Jossey-Bass Publishers, 1998.

Brueggemann, Walter. *Biblical Perspectives on Evangelism: Living in a Three-Storied Universe*. Nashville: Abingdon Press, 1993.

Carson, D.A. (ed.). *Telling the Truth, Evangelizing Postmoderns*. Grand Rapids: Zondervan, 2000.

Celek, Tim, and Dieter Zander, with Patrick Kampert. *Inside the Soul of a New Generation: Insights and Strategies for Reaching Busters*. Grand Rapids: Zondervan, 1996.

Coalter, Milton J., and Virgil Cruz (ed.). *How Shall We Witness? Faithful Evangelism in a Reformed Tradition*. Louisville: Westminster John Knox Press, 1995.

Craddock, Fred, B. *Overhearing the Gospel: Preaching and Teaching the Faith to Persons Who Have Heard It All Before*. Nashville: Abingdon Press, 1978.

Duern, Robert. *Conversion and the Catechumenate*. Mahwah, N.J.: Paulist Press, 1984.

Ford, Kevin Graham. *Jesus for a New Generation: Putting the Gospel in the Language of the Xers*. Downers Grove: InterVarsity Press, 1995.

Ford, Leighton. *The Power of Story: Rediscovering the Oldest, Most Natural Way to Reach People for Christ*. Colorado Springs: Nav Press, 1994.

Gelpi, Donald. *Committed Worship: A Sacramental Theology for Converting Christians, vol. 1—The Sacraments of Adult Conversion and Initiation*. Collegeville, Minn.: Liturgical Press, 1993.

Gumbel, Nicky. *The Alpha Course Video: A Practical Introduction to the Christian Faith*. Colorado Springs: Cook Communications Ministries, N.D.

Hahn, Todd, and David Verhaagen. *Gen Xers After God: Helping a Generation Pursue Jesus*. Grand Rapids: Baker, 1998.

Hybels, Bill, and Mark Mittelberg. *Becoming a Contagious Christian*. Grand Rapids: Zondervan, 1994.

Long, Jimmy. *Generating Hope: A Strategy for Reaching the Postmodern Generation*. Downers Grove: InterVarsity Press, 1997.

Mahedy, William, and Janet Bernard. *Generation Alone: Xers Making a Place in the World*. Downers Grove: InterVarsity Press, 1994.

Morgenthaller, Sally. *Worship Evangelism: Inviting Unbelievers into the Presence of God*. Grand Rapids: Zondervan, 1995.

Mittleberg, Mark. *Building a Contagious Church: Revolutionizing the Way We View and Do Evangelism*. Grand Rapids: Zondervan, 2000.

Newbigin, Lesslie. *Foolishness to the Greeks: The Gospel and Western Culture.* Grand Rapids: Eerdmans, 1986.

Pippert, Rebecca Manley. *Out to the Saltshaker and into the World: Evangelism as a Way of Life.* Downers Grove: InterVarsity Press, 1999. Second edition.

Richardson, Rick. *Evangelism Outside the Box: New Ways to Help People Experience the Good News.* Downers Grove: InterVarsity Press, 2000.

Riddell, Mike, Mark Pierson and Cathy Kirkpatrick. *The Prodigal Project: Journey into the Emerging Church.* London: SPCK, 2000.

Roxburgh, Alan J. *Reaching a New Generation: Strategies for Tomorrow's Church.* Vancouver: Regent College Publishing, 1998.

Sinwell, Joseph P. (ed.). *Come Follow Me: Resources for the Period of Inquiry in the RCIA.* Mahwah, N.J.: Paulist Press, 1990.

Sjogren, Steve. *Conspiracy of Kindness: A Refreshing New Approach to Sharing the Love of Jesus with Others.* Ann Arbor, Mich.: Servant Publications, 1993.

Strobel, Lee. *The Case for Christ.* Grand Rapids: Zondervan, 1998.

_____. *The Case for Faith.* Grand Rapids: Zondervan, 2000.

Wells, David. *God in the Wasteland: The Reality of Truth in a World of Fading Dreams.* Grand Rapids: Eerdmans, 1994.

Zoba, Wendy Murray. *Generation 2K: What Parents and Others Need to Know About the Millennials.* Downers Grove: InterVarsity Press, 1999.

PART III — DISCIPLING THE HEARER

Discipling the Hearer in the Early Church

Carrington, Phillip. *The Primitive Christian Catechism: A Study in the Epistles.* Cambridge: University Press, 1940.

Hall, Christopher A. *Reading Scriptures with the Church Fathers.* Downers Grove: InterVarsity Press, 1998.

Matsagouras, Elias. *The Early Church Fathers as Educators.* Minneapolis: Light and Life Publishing Co., 1977.

Discipling Today

Blackaby, Henry, T., and Claude V. King. *Experiencing God: How to Live the Full Adventure of Knowing and Doing the Will of God.* Nashville: Broadman & Holman Publishers, 1998.

Cary, James W. *Communication as Culture: Essays on Media and Society.* New York: Routledge, 1989.

Dominic F. Ashkar. *Road to Emmaus: A New Model for Catechesis.* San Jose, Calif.: Resource Publications, 1993.

Fowler, James W. *Becoming Adult, Becoming Christian: Adult Development and Christian Faith.* San Francisco: Jossey-Bass Publishers, 2000.

Groome, Thomas H. *Christian Religious Education: Sharing Our Story and Vision.* San Francisco: Harper & Row, 1980.

O'Donnell, James J. *Avatars of the Word: From Papyrus to Cyberspace.* Cambridge: Harvard University Press, 1998.

Palmer, Parker J. *To Know as We Are Known: Education as a Spiritual Journey.* San Francisco: HarperSanFrancisco, 1993.

Peterson, Eugene H. *A Long Obedience in the Same Direction: Discipleship in an Instant Society.* Downers Grove: InterVarsity Press, 1980.

Stock, Brian. *Listening for the Text: On the Uses of the Past.* Philadelphia: University of Pennsylvania Press, 1996.

Wilkins, Michael J. *Following the Master: A Biblical Theology of Discipleship.* Grand Rapids: Zondervan, 1992.

Vanier, Jean. *Becoming Human.* Toronto: House of Anansi Press Limited, 1998.

Williams, Clifford. *Singleness of Heart: Restoring the Divided Soul.* Grand Rapids: Eerdmans, 1994.

Discipling Through Rites and Stages

Eliade, Mircea. *Myth and Reality.* New York: Harper, 1963.

_____. *Rites and Symbols of Initiation: The Mysteries of Birth and Rebirth.* New York: Harper, 1958.

Fowler, James W. *Stages of Faith: The Psychology of Human Development and the Quest for Meaning.* San Francisco, HarperSanFrancisco, 1995.

Discipling Through Immersion in the Church

Hansen, David. *The Art of Pastoring: Ministry Without All the Answers.* Downers Grove: InterVarsity Press, 1994.

_____. *The Power of Loving Your Church: Leading Through Acceptance and Grace.* Minneapolis: Bethany House Publishers, 1998.

McMakin, Jacqueline, and Rhonda Nary. *Doorways to Christian Growth.* San Francisco: HarperSanFrancisco, 1984.

Mittleberg, Mark. *Building a Contagious Church: Revolutionizing the Way We View and Do Evangelism.* Grand Rapids: Zondervan, 2000.

Morris, Thomas H. *The RCIA: Transforming the Church: A Resource for Pastoral Implementation.* Mahwah, N.J.: Paulist Press, 1997. Revised and updated version.

Pohl, Christine D. *Making Room: Recovering Christian Hospitality as a Christian Tradition*. Grand Rapids: Eerdmans, 1999.

Discipling with a Spiritual Mentor

Merton, Thomas. *Spiritual Direction and Meditation*. Collegeville, Minn.: Liturgical Press, 1960.
Nemeck, Francis Kelly. *The Way of Spiritual Direction*. Collegeville, Minn.: Liturgical Press, 1985.

Discipling Through the Small Group Ministry

Galloway, Dale, with Keith Mills. *The Small Group Book: The Practical Guide for Nurturing Christians and Building Churches*. Grand Rapids: Baker, 1995.
Henderson, Michael D. *John Wesley's Class Meetings: A Model for Making Disciples*. Nappanee, Ind.: Evangel Publishing House, 1997.
Icenogle, Gareth Weldon. *Biblical Foundations for Small Group Ministry: An Integrational Approach*. Downers Grove: InterVarsity Press, 1994.
Wuthnow, Robert (ed.). *"I Come Away Stronger": How Small Groups Are Shaping American Religion*. Grand Rapids: Eerdmans, 1994.
Volf, Miroslav. *After Our Likeness: The Church as the Image of the Trinity*. Grand Rapids: Eerdmans, 1998.

Discipling Through Worship

Dawn, J. Marva. *Reaching Out Without Dumbing Down: A Theology of Worship for the Turn-of-the-Century Culture*. Grand Rapids: Eerdmans, 1995.
————. *A Royal "Waste" of Time: The Splendor of Worshiping God and Being Church*. Grand Rapids: Eerdmans, 1995.
Gelpi, Donald L. *Committed Worship: A Sacramental Theology for Converting Christians, vol. 2—The Sacraments of Ongoing Conversion*. Collegeville, Minn.: Liturgical Press, 1993.
Neville, Gwen Kennedy, and John H. Westerhoff III. *Learning Through the Liturgy*. New York: Seabury Press, 1978.
Schattauer, Thomas H. (ed.). *Inside Out: Worship in an Age of Mission*. Philadelphia: Fortress Press, 2000.
Torrance, James B. *Worship Community and the Triune God of Grace*. Downers Grove: InterVarsity Press, 1996.
Westerhoff, John H. III, and William Willimon. *Liturgy and Learning Through the Life Cycle*. Akron, Ohio: OSL Publications, 1980, 1994.

Discipling Through Scripture

Anderson, Bernard W. *The Unfolding Drama of the Bible: Eight Studies Introducing the Bible as a Whole*. Philadelphia: Fortress Press, 1988.

Childs, Brevard S. *Old Testament Theology in a Canonical Context*. Philadelphia: Fortress Press, 1985.

Ewart, David. *How to Understand the Bible*. Scottdale, Penn.: Herald Press, 2000.

Fee, Gordon, and Douglas Stuart. *How to Read the Bible for All Its Worth: A Guide to Understanding the Bible*. Grand Rapids: Zondervan, 1993. Second edition.

Hall, Thelma. *Too Deep for Words: Rediscovering Lectio Divina*. Mahwah, N.J.: Paulist Press, 1988.

Hauerwas, Stanley, and L. Gregory Jones. *Why Narrative? Readings in Narrative Theology*. Eugene, Ore.: Wipf & Stock Publishers, 1997.

Lodal, Michael. *The Story of God: Wesleyan Theology and Biblical Narrative*. Kansas City: Beach Hill Press, 1994.

Muto, Susan Anette. *A Practical Guide to Spiritual Reading*. Petersham, Mass.: St. Bede's, 1994.

Pennington, Basil M. *Lectio Divina: Renewing the Ancient Practice of Praying the Scripture*. New York: Crossroad Publishing, 1998.

Ricoeur, Paul. *Essays on Biblical Interpretation*. Philadelphia: Fortress, 1980.

IV. EQUIPPING THE KNEELER

Spirituality Within the Ancient Church

A Way of Desert Spirituality: The Plan of Life of the Hermits of Bethlehem. New York: Alda House, 1988. Revised edition.

Meyendorff, John. *St. Gregory Palamas and Orthodox Spirituality*. Crestwood, N.Y.: St. Vladimir's Seminary Press, 1974.

Russell, Norman (trans.) *The Lives of the Desert Fathers: The Historia Monoachorum in Aegypto*. Oxford: Cistercian Publications, 1980.

Spirituality in General

Allen, Joseph J. *Inner Way: Toward a Rebirth of Eastern Christian Spiritual Direction*. Grand Rapids: Eerdmans, 1994.

Byrne, Lavinia (ed.). *Traditions of Spiritual Guidance: Collected from "The Way"*. Collegeville: Liturgical Press, 1990.

Chambers, Oswald. *Christian Disciplines.* Grand Rapids: Discovery House Publishers, 1936, 1995.

Collins, Kenneth J. (ed.). *Exploring Christian Spirituality: An Ecumenical Reader.* Grand Rapids: Baker, 2000.

French, R.M. (ed.). *The Way of a Pilgrim and the Pilgrim Continues His Way.* New York: Crossroad, 1965.

Jones, Cheslyn, Geoffrey Wainwright, and Edward Yarnold, S.J. *The Study of Spirituality.* New York: Oxford, 1986.

Jones, Paul W. *A Season in the Desert: Making Time Holy.* Orleans, Mass.: Paraclete Press, 2000.

Macaulay, Ranald, and Jerram Barrs. *Being Human: The Nature of Spiritual Experience.* Downers Grove: InterVarsity Press, 1978.

McGrath, Alister E. *Christian Spirituality.* Malden, Mass.: Blackwell Publishers, 1999.

Peterson, Eugene H. *Subversive Spirituality.* Grand Rapids: Eerdmans, 1994, 1997.

Piper, John. *God's Passion for His Glory: Living the Vision of Jonathan Edwards, with the Complete Text of the End for Which God Created the World.* Wheaton, Ill.: Crossway Books, 1998.

Powell, Samuel M., and Michael E. Lodahl (eds). *Embodied Holiness: Toward a Corporate Theology of Spiritual Growth.* Downers Grove: InterVarsity Press, 1999.

Schroeder, Celeste Snowbar. *In the Womb of God: Creative Nurture for the Soul.* Liguori, Mo.: Triumph Books, 1995.

Webber, Robert. *The Prymer: The Prayer Book of the Medieval Era Adapted for Contemporary Use.* Orleans, Mass.: Paraclete Press, 2000.

Whitlock, Luder G. *The Spiritual Quest: Pursuing Christian Maturity.* Grand Rapids: Baker, 2000.

Willard, Dallas. *The Divine Conspiracy: Rediscovering Our Hidden Life in God.* San Francisco, HarperSanFrancisco, 1998.

_____. *The Spirit of the Disciplines: Understanding How God Changes Lives.* San Francisco: HarperSanFrancisco, 1991.

_____. *Hearing God: Developing a Conversational Relationship with God.* Downers Grove: InterVarsity Press, 1984, 1993, 1999.

Spiritual Warfare

Aulén, Gustaf. *Christus Victor: An Historical Study of the Three Main Types of the Idea of the Atonement.* Macmillan Company, 1969.

Boyd, Gregory A. *God at War: The Bible and Spiritual Conflict.* Downers Grove: InterVarsity Press, 1997.

Braaten, Carl E., and Robert W. Jenson (eds). *Sin, Death, and the Devil.* Grand Rapids: Eerdmans, 2000.

Hauerwas, Stanley, and William Willimon. *The Truth About God: The Ten Commandments in Christian Life*. Nashville: Abingdon Press, 1999.

Nicodemus of the Holy Mountain (ed.); and revised by Theophan the Recluse. *Unseen Warfare*. Crestwood, N.Y.: St. Vladimir's Seminary Press, 1995.

Sweet, Leonard. *Learning to Dance the Soul Salsa: 17 Surprising Steps for Godly Living in the 21st Century*. Grand Rapids: Zondervan, 2000.

Wink, Walter. *Naming the Powers: The Language of Power in the New Testament*. Philadelphia: Fortress Press, 1984.

_____. *Unmasking the Powers: The Invisible Forces That Determine Human Existence*. Philadelphia: Fortress Press, 1986.

_____. *Engaging the Powers: Discernment and Resistance in a World of Domination*. Philadelphia: Fortress Press, 1992.

Zacharias, Ravi. *Deliver Us from Evil: Restoring the Soul in a Disintegrating Culture*. Nashville: Word, 1997.

Spirituality of the Christian Life (Virtue)

Foster, Richard J., and Jana Rea. *A Spiritual Formation Journal: A Renovaré Resource for Spiritual Renewal*. San Francisco: HarperSanFrancisco, 1996.

Guroian, Vigen. *Ethics After Christendom, Toward an Ecclesial Christian Ethic*. Grand Rapids: Eerdmans, 1994.

Hauerwas, Stanley, and Charles Pinches. *Christians Among the Virtues: Theological Conversations with Ancient and Modern Ethics*. Notre Dame: University of Notre Dame Press, 1977.

_____. *A Community of Character: Toward a Constructive Christian Social Ethic*. Notre Dame: University of Notre Dame Press, 1981.

Kenneson, Philip D. *Life on the Vine: Cultivating the Fruit of the Spirit in Christian Community*. Downers Grove: InterVarsity Press, 1999.

Nouwen, Henri J. M. *The Way of the Heart: Desert Spirituality and Contemporary Ministry*. San Francisco: Harper, 1981.

Pieper, Jose F. *A Brief Reader on the Virtues of the Human Heart*. San Francisco: Ignatius, 1986.

Wells, David F. *Losing Our Virtue: Why the Church Must Recover Its Moral Vision*. Grand Rapids: Eerdmans, 1998.

Spirituality of Prayer

Ebeling, Gerhard. *The Lord's Prayer*. Orleans, Mass.: Paraclete Press, 1999.

Foster, Richard J. *Prayer: Finding the Hearts True Home*. San Francisco: HarperSanFrancisco, 1992.

Hauerwas, Stanley, Scott Saye, and William Willimon. *Lord Teach Us: The Lord's Prayer and the Christian Life*. Nashville: Abingdon Press, 1996.

Herman, Arigio, E. Edited by Hal M. Helms. *Creative Prayer*. Orleans, Mass.: Paraclete Press, 1998.

Kneeft, Peter. *Prayer for Beginners*. San Francisco: Ignatius Press, 2000.

Martin, Linette. *Practical Praying*. Grand Rapids, Eerdmans, 1997.

Saliers, Don E. *The Soul in Paraphrase: Prayer and the Religious Affections*. Cleveland: OSL Publications, 1980, 1991.

Schroeder, Celeste Snowber. *Embodied Prayer: Harmonizing Body and Soul*. Liguori, Mo.: Triumph Books, 1995.

Von Balthasar, Hans U. *Prayer*. San Francisco: Ignatius, 1986.

Spirituality of the Creed

Sayers, Dorothy L. *Creed or Chaos?* Manchester, N.H.: Sophia Institute Press, 1949, 1974.

Simpson, Gregory, Brother, *The Nicene Creed for Today*, Orleans, Mass.: Paraclete Press, 1999.

V. INCORPORATING THE FAITHFUL

Gifts in the Early Church

Wehrli, Eugene S. *Gifted by Their Spirit: Leadership Roles in the New Testament*. Cleveland: The Pilgrim Press, 1992.

Gifts in the Church Today

Countryman, William L. *Living on the Border of the Holy: Renewing the Priesthood of All*. Harrisburg, Penn.: Morehouse Publishing, 1999.

Christensen, Michael J., and Carl Savage (eds). *Equipping the Saints: Mobilizing Laity for Ministry for Ministry*. Nashville: Abingdon Press, 2000.

Cullinan, Alice, R. *Sorting It Out: Discerning God's Call to Ministry*. Valley Forge: Judson Press, 1999.

Davis, Kortright. *Serving with Power: Reviving the Spirit of Christian Ministry*. Mahwah, N.J.: Paulist Press, 1999.

Donnelly, Doris (ed.). *Retrieving Charisms for the Twenty-First Century*. Collegeville: Minn.: Liturgical Press, 1999.

Fortune, Don and Katie. *Discover Your God Given Gifts*. Grand Rapids: Baker, 1987.

Henricksen, Walter A. *Disciples Are Made Not Born: Equipping Christians to Multiply Themselves Through Ministry to Others*. Colorado Springs: Cook Communications, 1974, 1988.

Ogden, Greg. *The New Reformation: Returning the Ministry to the People of God*. Grand Rapids: Zondervan, 1990.

Osborne, Kenan B. OFM, *Ministry: Lay Ministry in the Roman Catholic Church: Its History and Theology*. Mahwah, N.Y.: Paulist Press, 1993.

Paprocki, Joe. *You Give Them Something to Eat: Ministering When You Think You Can't*. Notre Dame, Ind.: Ave Maria Press, 2000.

Quinn, Robert E. *Deep Change: Discovering the Leader Within*. San Francisco: Jossey-Bass Publishers, 1996.

Sanford, Agnes. *The Healing Gifts of the Spirit*. Philadelphia: Lippincott, 1966.

Sofield, Loughlan, ST, and Carroll Juliano, SHCJ. *Collaboration: Uniting Our Gifts in Ministry*. Notre Dame, Ind.: Ave Maria Press, 2000.

Stevens, Paul R. *Liberating the Laity: Equipping All the Saints for Ministry*. Vancouver: Regent College Publishing, 1993.

_____. *The Other Six Days: Vocation Work and Ministry in Biblical Perspective*. Grand Rapids: Eerdmans, 1999.

Spirituality of the Eucharist

Bodey, Richard Allen, and Robert Leslie Holmes (eds). *Come to the Banquet: Meditations for the Lord's Table*. Grand Rapids: Baker, 1998.

Kass, Leon, R., M.D. *The Hungry Soul: Eating and the Perfecting of Our Nature*. Chicago: University of Chicago Press, 1994, 1999.

Macy, Gary. *The Banquet's Wisdom: A Short History of the Theologies of the Lord's Supper*.

Rordorff, Willy, et al. *The Eucharist of the Early Christians*. New York: Pueblo Publishing Company, 1978.

Schmemann, Alexander. *The Eucharist: Sacrament of the Kingdom*. Crestwood, N.Y.: St. Vladimir's Press, 1988.

Zizioulas, John D. *Being as Communion: Studies in Personhood and the Church*. Crestwood, N.Y.: St. Vladimir's Press, 1997.

New Members Sharing Christ

Greene, Michael. *One to One: How to Share Your Faith with a Friend*. Nashville: Moorings, 1995.

_____. *Evangelism Through the Local Church*. London: Hodder & Stoughton, 1990.

_____. *How Can I Lead a Friend to Christ? A Practical Guide to Personal Evangelism*. London: Hodder & Stoughton, 1995.

Hybels, Bill, and Mark Mittelberg. *Becoming a Contagious Christian*. Grand Rapids: Zondervan, 1994.